The Liberation of Pointe du Hoc

The 2nd U.S. Rangers at Normandy

by JoAnna McDonald

Rank and File PUBLICATIONS

1926 South Pacific Coast Highway Suite 228
Redondo Beach, California 90277

A battlefield grave site of a 2d Ranger at Pointe-du-Hoc, June '44.
Lou Lisko's Ranger Box, USAMHI

Publisher's Cataloging-in-Publication

McDonald, JoAnna M., 1970 -
       The Liberation of Pointe du Hoc : the 2nd U.S. Rangers at
       Normandy / by JoAnna McDonald. --1st ed. p. cm.
       Includes bibliographical references and index.
       ISBN: 1-888967-06-4

       1, World War, 1939-1945--Campaigns--France--Normandy--
       --Pictorial works. 2. United States Army Ranger Battalion,
       2nd--History. 3. Operation Overlord. 4. Normandy
       (France)--History, Military.
       D756.5.N6M33 1998   940.54'2142

Table of Contents

Preface

The Ranger Battle Honors Flag

The Ranger Battalions' Battle Honors Flag represents the proud and enduring record of the Six United States Army Ranger Battalions in World War II. The Rangers of all six battalions are equally as proud of the achievements of each and every Ranger Battalion as they are of their own.

The Ranger philosophy for winning battles was tough, realistic battle training, inspired leadership, detailed planning, thorough reconnaissance, contact, coordination and control, hit the enemy where he least expects it, choose the most difficult route of approach, attack at night with speed, surprise and shock, carry through relentlessly. These concepts were proven in battle after battle.

The record speaks for itself. The Rangers spearheaded every Major Invasion of World War II — the first to land, the first to die, the first to capture the enemy's defenses and make it possible for other troops to land and broaden the beachheads. Fifteen campaigns, innumerable battles and engagements, raids and sorties — and who can keep track of the countless combat patrols and night infiltrations that were never mentioned in the daily communiques?

But the Battle Records of the Six Army Ranger Battalions do not tell the full story of the American Ranger in World War II. The spirit that each Ranger carried in his breast — that drove him to accomplish the impossible, that inspired him to attack the most formidable enemy defenses, that enabled him to endure in campaign after campaign, that compelled him to excel as an American soldier, this is the most important part of the Ranger story that is represented on our Battle Honors Flag.

We, who were privileged to have served with the Rangers, know what that spirit was. It was a spirit that was formed by many essential elements. Leadership by example, mutual respect and esteem, concern for our fellow Ranger, teamwork, pride in our units, a comprehension of why we were fighting, the will to win, not at all cost, but by skill, preparation and ingenuity. The Ranger spirit was a mixture of individuality tempered by self discipline and directed toward the achievement of the common objectives of victory. The Ranger spirit was audacity and daring and originality. It was resourcefulness and versatility. It was a positive force. It was, in essence, the spirt that has kept liberty alive since time immemorial — the willingness to give of yourself to a common cause — above and beyond the call of duty — above and beyond one's obligation as an Amerlcan cltlzen.

The Ranger spirit is an important part of our national heritage, and each Ranger who fought with the Six Ranger Battalions, helped make that heritage stronger and significant. We are mindful that we, as custodians of that spirit, have a serious obligation not only to keep that spirit alive, but to keep it vigorous and strong and direct that spirit towards positive good for our country today.

James Altieri, 1st and 4th Ranger Battalions
Past President
Ranger Bns. Association WWII

A time to be born and a time to die
A time to kill and a time to heal,
A time to weep and a time to laugh
A time to love and a time to hate,
A time for war and a time for peace ...
---Ecclesiastes 3:2-8

BECAUSE

They acknowledged the Providence, the Mercy, the Justice of God;
BECAUSE
They gave that last measure of devotion for their country;
BECAUSE
They loved their Homes and died to keep them safe;
BECAUSE
They shall be our inspiration to make this Peace, a lasting Peace;

and

BECAUSE
They were our Ranger brothers, the Second Ranger Battalion respectfully commends this
book to honor the Battalion's heroic dead.*

Respectfully submitted,

Leonard G. Lomell
Co. D, 2d Ranger Battalion

*Another version of this dedication can be found in *Ranger Battalion: The Narrative History of Headquarter's Company, April 1943-May 1, 1945*

Introduction

"Destroy the 155mm guns, set up roadblocks, and disrupt and destroy the German communications," Lt. Col. James Earl Rudder, commanding officer of the 2d Ranger Battalion, thought to himself as his LCA (Landing Craft Assault boat) raced toward the Normandy coast on June 6, 1944. The Allied commanders had given him only 225 Rangers to successfully complete this three-pronged mission. The suppression of the guns at Pointe-du-Hoc could literally make a life or death difference to the U.S. troops landing on Omaha and Utah Beaches. It was a heavy responsibility and a dangerous and difficult job, but Rudder and his men had all volunteered.

The Rangers had trained for two years; they were the *crème de la crème*. They had endured extreme physical training and had climbed numerable, unforgiving cliffs in the United States, England and Scotland. Now the big show was on, and many of them were sick. The combination of rough seas and raw nerves had unsettled their stomachs. Soldiers began vomiting on themselves and their comrades. The bottom of the boats were filling with water and puke. Rangers found themselves soaked through; the waves rocked their vessels like tin cans in a cyclone. To many it seemed they might never even reach the shore — some would not.

In the lead vessel, LCA 888, Col. Rudder wiped the ocean spray out of his eyes and squinted toward land. As the boat sped closer, the colonel realized the coxswain was headed toward Pointe-de-la-Percee, half-way between Pointe-du-Hoc and the Vierville draw. Rudder yelled to the British coxswain and convinced him to turn right.

This error cost the 2d Ranger Battalion 35 minutes and caused them to travel 200-300 yards parallel to the beach. The Germans perched high on cliffs had observed the small armada running the gauntlet of their fire. As the Rangers approached, enemy machine-gunners loaded their weapons; an officer yelled, "*Schießen!*"

All hell broke loose as 20mm cannon fire tore through the column. Huge holes were made in the thin-skinned boats. Bullets and artillery fire exploded close to the LCAs. Rudder's Rangers were sitting ducks. With hearts pounding, some prayed; others focused on the job ahead.

Once near the shore, enraged Rangers stood up in their boats and blasted the Germans. While landing, officers ordered the rockets carrying the ropes to be fired. Many ropes failed to reach the cliffs, either because they were water-logged or because they were fired too early. Enough did lodge, however, to carry the men to the top. With the rockets and ropes let loose, the ramps on the boats went down; men rushed across the narrow beach. They grabbed the first rope they saw and began to climb. In about 15 minutes 180 of the 225 rugged Rangers ascended the precipice, ready for their three-part mission which lay ahead.

* * * *

England and France had waited five long, trying years for June 6, 1944, D-Day. The Allies had been battling Adolph Hitler's Third Reich since 1939. In 1940 Great Britain and the remnants of the French Armies were forced out of France. The situation was grim as England withstood night after night of air attacks. But Hitler and his *Luftwaffe* generals underestimated the headstrong Brits; they would not concede. They pledged to fight to the last.

The United States had been carefully watching the war in Europe. At first President Franklin D. Roosevelt and Congress refrained from dispatching large groups of Army personnel, but they did send supplies, and secretly sent American pilots, to Great Britain.

On December 7, 1941, Imperial Japan's sudden and unprovoked attack on the U.S. Naval base at Pearl Harbor transformed the dynamics of the conflict. Immediately, the United States declared war on Japan and Germany.

From the start, Allied commanders intended to return to France and thwart Hitler's plan for world domination. Devising a strategy for the great invasion, however, was not an easy task. Three years passed before the Allies felt confident enough to strike the Atlantic Wall. General Dwight D. Eisenhower, supreme commander of all Allied Forces in Europe, along with his generals, organized and designed the largest invasion ever seen in military history.

To prepare for this landing, several years earlier, the Allies established entire units to be trained for specialized missions. The 2d Rangers were one of those battalions and were officially organized and activated on April 1, 1943. Many would drop out due to injuries, death, and the physical extremes demanded of the job; their bodies were taken to the breaking point. Those who made it through were prepared to withstand the worst. And here they were, two years after they had begun their training, the 2d Rangers playing out their role in history.

D-Day was scheduled to commence on June 5, 1944, but was delayed for one day due to bad weather. Eisenhower gave the "go" for June 6th. In one night and day, June 5-6, 175,000 soldiers were transported across the English Channel to France. Approximately 5,333 ships and 11,000 airplanes participated in this famed assault.[1]

The planners divided the Normandy coast into five significant beach landings. The Americans fought on Utah and Omaha Beaches; the English landed on Sword and Gold, and the Canadians came in on Juno Beach. Between Omaha and Utah beaches lay Pointe-du-Hoc. Rising approximately 100 feet, it was a prominent position. Near the bluff the Germans deployed six huge 155mm cannon with which to enfilade Omaha and Utah beaches. Their range was approximately 25,000 yards — or ten miles. With these guns the Germans could not only destroy any infantry attempting to take the beaches, but the landing craft in the Channel as well. A crack unit was needed to accomplish the impossible: climb the heights and take out the guns.

For this task Eisenhower chose Companies D, E, and F and part of Headquarters Company of the 2d Ranger Battalion, about 225 men. They would ascend the cliff, destroy the huge guns deployed in casemates (armored gun enclosures), set up roadblocks, break up German communications, and hold back any counterattacks.

To help soften the German entrenchments prior to the landing, the Allied Navy and Army Air Corps bombed the trenches along the coast. The bombing of Pointe-du-Hoc, however, had begun several weeks prior to June 6. American and British bombers had saturated the area, and just prior to H-hour, 6:30 a.m., huge Naval guns aboard the *Texas* pummeled it once again for good measure. When given the order to go, the Rangers, in British LCAs, headed for shore.

* * * *

This is their story. Using photographs, maps, first-hand accounts and secondary sources the reader will conceptualize the tremendous struggle that occurred at Pointe-du-Hoc some 55 years ago. We will look at the 2d Ranger Battalion's training and a detailed account of some of the individuals who volunteered for this renowned outfit.

One should note, however, that not all of the survivors interviewed agree on the times and layout of the events. Most combat veterans admit that no single participant can ever fully sketch the constant shifting of the bloody panorama which we call a battle. Nevertheless, these conflicting viewpoints did not affect the telling of the story and are addressed in the endnotes.

The Liberation of Pointe-du-Hoc remains the pivotal battle in which the Rangers earned their reputation as one of the most elite commando units in military history.

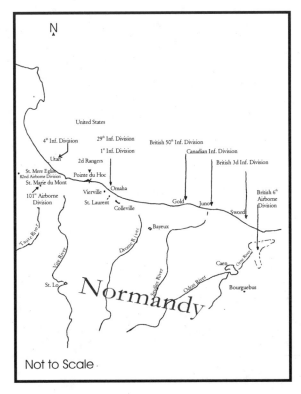

Map 1

The Allies landed on five beaches on D-Day. The German battery at Pointe-du-Hoc lay between Utah and Omaha beaches. If the guns were not silenced the enemy could have destroyed the U.S. infantry hitting these sectors and the Naval armada lying 12 miles off the Normandy coast.

oniente-du-Hoc from the air
Note the numerous shell craters caused by the Air Corps bombs.
Photo taken circa 1944.
Louis Lisko Coll., Ranger Box, USAMHI

East side of Pointe du Hoc

Notes for Introduction

[1] D-Day Memorial Pamphlet text, printed by the members of the D-Day Memorial Foundation. D-Day was the military term designated for any day for which an invasion was planned to commence. The invasion of Sicily, for example, had its D-Day. The June 6, 1944, battle, however, was so immense in scope and so historically pivotal that it has come to be known as *the* "D-Day."

Acknowledgments

Throughout the process of successfully researching a book of this magnitude I was warmly received and encouraged by many veterans, librarians, archivists and D-Day centers.

My family also played a role, especially my Dad who bought me all the books on military subjects I could devour as a young child and who served in the 7th Special Forces, 1961-1964.

Mom worked hard as one of my editors. As always, she showed great support while patiently reading and rereading numerous drafts. Suse Fruhhaber also helped with the spelling of the German words used herein, and Ann Masland worked on the maps.

As a military historian it was an honor to speak with and actually meet some of Rudder's Rangers. Those 2d Ranger Veterans with whom I was able to make contact happily came to my assistance: James W. Eikner, HQ Company; Gene Elder, F-Co.; George Kerchner, D Company; Jack Kuhn, D Company; Len Lomell, D Company; Herman Stein, F Company; and Bill Walsh, F Company. They all provided fact editing and contributed information to ensure the accuracy of the story of the 2d Rangers at Pointe-du-Hoc. For their dedication to service, their deeds and faces will be remembered for many years to come. I thank them for their devotion and sacrifice which made it possible for my generation of Americans to live in freedom. I am indebted, also, to the wives of many Veterans who helped them to gather and supply documents for this effort.

Lou Lisko's work (HQ Company and former 2d Ranger historian) helped me sort through the details. Lou passed away in August 1998, but, prior to his death, he made his information available by donating many of his papers and photographs to the United States Army Military History Institute in Carlisle.

Archives and libraries around the country supplied letters, oral histories and memoirs. Annie Wedkind, assistant director of the Eisenhower Center, and their intern, Michael Edwards, contributed many valuable oral histories of Ranger veterans from their vast collection. As always, the staff of the Military History Institute, Carlisle Barracks, Pennsylvania, provided guidance and friendship: John Slonaker and Louise Arnold-Friend, reference historians, Dave Keough and Pam Chaney, archivists; and last, but not least, Michael Winey and Randy Hackenburg, Photo Archivists. The staff at the National Archives, and Mike Duggan, Archivist at President Ronald Reagan's library, sent several documents concerning Pointe-du-Hoc.

Lastly, I would like to thank Richard Rollins, Rank and File Publications, for giving me the opportunity to write this book and to learn more about these American heroes.

Chapter 1

"The Super-trained Fighting Man":
Those That Came Before

The term "ranger" was not new to military history in 1944. Its roots lay in the woodlands of England and the New World. Derived from the Frankish word "hring," which meant circle or ring,[1] in the Americas the term was associated with hardy frontiersmen. These rangers played a significant role in early battles between white settlers and Native Americans.

Rather than meet an enemy, who often outnumbered them, head-on (European style), the Indians ambushed their opponents and conducted hit-and-run raids against isolated forts, farms and trade posts. Since the posts and forts were usually built miles apart, native war parties could easily move undetected between them. Consequently, European factions hired rangers to patrol the unsettled area surrounding the far-flung outposts. These men were primarily professional soldiers or qualified militiamen.[2] Most of the time they were "mounted troops... armed with short muskets, who ranged over the country, often fighting on foot."[3]

One of America's first rangers of note, Robert Rogers, led his New Hampshire pioneersmen into the wilderness. In 1755, after Indians ambushed Maj. Gen. Edward Braddock's expedition and nearly wiped it out, the British saw the necessity for utilizing frontiersmen as scouts. Robert Rogers was first hired to reconnoiter during the winter of 1755-56. Throughout the French and Indian War he and his men continued to scout and raid for the British.

Governor William Shirley of Massachusetts noted Rogers' work and invited him to Boston in March 1756. Shirley and Rogers discussed the role of rangers in an army. The governor recognized the need for men who could locate routes, gather intelligence, and conduct raids against enemy ammunition dumps and settlements. As a result of this conversation, Rogers received a commission as captain and led a 60-man ranger team. Individual rangers were chosen based on their skill in woodcraft and marksmanship.[4]

While the British preferred to use Rogers' Rangers as scouts, the rangers successfully participated in offensive missions as well. They harassed French communications along the western shore of Lake Champlain; they destroyed several supply convoys; they captured prisoners, and raided Indian villages. After the war, Rogers' Rangers were dissolved, and Rogers was left without retirement pay or rank; however, during the American Revolution he raised a battalion of Loyalist rangers for the British — the Queen's American Rangers.

In addition to Rogers' unit, Col. John Butler's Loyalist Rangers fought for the British Army. Cooperating with the Indians, these units terrorized American settlers in New York and Pennsylvania. After the war both countries continued to use rangers as scouts and guardians of the frontier.[5]

The most infamous Colonial rangers during the American Revolution were Morgan's Rangers. In 1775 Congress called for volunteer riflemen from Pennsylvania, Maryland, and Virginia. Capt. Daniel Morgan recruited a company from Virginia. Morgan's men dressed in hunting shirts, wore coon skin caps, carried tomahawks, knives, and shouldered long rifles. They were a rowdy and tough group, and Morgan was fearless. His company served as scouts and flank guards during the Quebec march. Captain Morgan and most of his men were captured when the attempt to capture that city failed. Returned in a prisoner exchange, Morgan gathered another group of volunteers and rejoined the Continental Army. At this time their job included scouting, guarding roads and harassing the enemy. Morgan's Rangers, however, were not the only American ranger battalion during those years.

In 1776 Lt. Col. Thomas Knowlton, from Connecticut, enlisted men from Massachusetts and Connecticut to form a battalion of light infantrymen. Knowlton's Rangers fought well in the battle of Harlem Heights in September of 1776, but Knowlton was mortally wounded. In November the British captured most of Knowlton's men at Fort Washington.[6]

Almost 50 years later, Stephen Austin, in 1823 when Texas was still under Mexico's rule, called for a ranger unit to help them fight for their freedom from Mexico. The rugged Texans provided their own horses and firearms. They carried long rifles, shotguns, and adopted the Colt six-shooter. John C. Hays and Ben McCulloch became two of the rangers' best known leaders. After Texas won independence from Mexico, rangers were called upon once more in the Mexican War (1846-1848). During this conflict Maj. Gen. Zachary Taylor utilized the Texas Rangers as scouts and guides.[7]

Thirteen years later, during the American Civil War, the South called upon rangers to serve their cause. At least 400 ranger-style units participated in the Civil War from 1861-1865. Confederate John S. Mosby probably became the most legendary ranger of the war. In January, 1863, Maj. Gen. Jeb Stuart ordered Mosby to take nine men and conduct operations in the Union rear. The expedition succeeded, and Mosby won a commission as a captain of partisan rangers. Mosby's Rangers carried out hundreds of hit-and-run operations against the Union armies in Virginia. They also destroyed supply trains, captured couriers, and generally harassed the Yankees in any way they could. Out in Texas, the Texas Rangers once again formed to fight the Federal armies.[8]

. . .

The U.S. Army did not utilize rangers again until 1942. The concept resurfaced following the publicity of the British commandos. In 1940 the British and French armies retreated in front of the German advance. They fled to Dunkirk and then back to England. The English Channel separating large land forces created a need to conduct amphibious warfare. Small groups of raiders could secretly land anywhere along the German-held coastline — from Navik to Bordeaux.[9] As a result of Lt. Col. Dudley Clarke's recommendation, Winston Churchill approved the formation of a guerrilla force. They termed these men "Commandos." From the beginning Churchill insisted that these forces take the offensive. The Prime Minister suggested that the units conduct amphibious operations, destroy strategic targets, and quickly return home. The special force would essentially initiate a reign of terror against the Germans.[10]

Winston Churchill soon broadened his goals for these commandos and wrote to the Chief of Staff for the Ministry of Defense on June 6, 1940:

> The passive-resistance war, in which we have acquitted
> ourselves so well, must come to an end. I look to the Joint Chiefs
> of Staff to propose measures for vigourous, enterprising, and

ceaseless offensive against the whole German occupied coastline.[11]

The Prime Minister persisted in encouraging the formation of the special strike force, and the British finally began organizing commando units in June 1940.[12]

Training included a variety of skills: exercises in small boats during all types of weather, swimming, a thorough knowledge of weapons and explosives, and tank killer techniques. Physical conditioning was vital to the commandos' program. Long marches were often on the agenda, and swimming or crossing a river with toggle ropes was not unusual. The British also concentrated on scaling and climbing cliffs since such obstacles were often a part of an amphibious landing.[13]

Commandos underwent live-fire training while maneuvering through obstacle courses. In addition, the British took great care to focus on self-reliance and self-confidence to ensure that each soldier would be able to use his initiative and innovative powers to the fullest.[14]

In July, 1940, Admiral Lord Keyes became the Director of Combined Operations. Keyes wanted to conduct large scale assaults involving thousands of soldiers rather than small, elite operations. Consequently, he was replaced by Lord Mountbatten. Under Mountbatten, commando raids began to increase. Their operations included attacks on shipping and factories in Guernsey, the Lofoten Islands, Norway, Vaagso, St. Nazaire, Boulogne, North Africa and Sicily.[15] The British raids were not only militarily useful, they helped raise the morale of civilian and military personnel alike.

As the commando raids increased in popularity so, too, did their notoriety across the Atlantic Ocean. Their courageous deeds were described in notable American magazines and newspapers. The *New York Times* magazine described the commandos as "super-guerrillas, the modern Apaches of the British Army. They are a tough, hard-trained, ruthless hit and run corps, the pick of the dare devils of the modern armies."[16]

Bruce Thomas in his article, "The Commando," characterized them as

> ...the super-trained fighting man — a combination of Peck's Bad Boy, Robin Hood, Tarzan, a first-class Boy Scout, Superman, and Daniel Boone. He is the cagiest and canniest fighting man on the loose to-day. His average age is twenty-seven ...the world's number one guerrilla fighters and unconventional scouts. Every man has been hand-picked for the job...These modern raiders are physically on their toes. They have to be. Their job means that they must be topnotch participants in all branches of sports.[17]

Once America declared war on the Axis Powers in 1941, the United States began to mobilize thousands of men for military service. After a year of building its forces, Gen. George C. Marshall, U.S. Armed Forces Chief of Staff, sent a memorandum to President Franklin D. Roosevelt endorsing the establishment of commando-style units.

In order to study British commando operations, Marshall sent Gen. Lucian K. Truscott, Jr., along with other American officers, to England. Truscott's main objective was to arrange for an American presence in these British raids thus giving the United States some battle experience. While in England, Truscott began asking British officers their opinions of these commando units. Many officers expressed their opposition stating that they had lost some of their best men in recruitment for the formation of these groups. Other men complained that too much publicity had been given to the commandos, and the morale among the other troops was low. General Truscott's findings also disclosed that American officers tended to agree with the British criticism.[18]

Despite the fact that some officers held negative opinions concerning the genesis of commando units, Truscott remained steadfast in his belief that an American version of this special force should be organized. In addition, he felt they should be established using the British Commandos as their model. Truscott submitted his proposal on May 26, 1942:

> ...we should form a unit organization along the lines which the British had found desirable, rather than utilize a regular formation whose organization would have to be modified for every operation. Through such a unit, personnel could be rotated as men gained battle experience, with fewer complications than would be the case if men were transferred away from old organizations.[19]

General Marshall agreed with Truscott's proposal and, on May 27, outlined his plan to form the first American Commando unit. Approximately 35 officers and 450 men, all hand-picked, would be sent to England to endure the rigors of the British commando training camp. Maj. Gen. James E. Chaney, who had been assigned as a United States military observer in Britain prior to America's entrance into the war and who later became commander of United States' build-up forces in Britain, in a letter written June 1, 1942, stressed that the soldiers selected must be trained at the

highest caliber. In addition, they should be "intelligent and in good health and physical condition without any defects. Personnel selected should be capable of maximum exertion and endurance expected of men of that age [25]."[20] Preference was also given to those expert in "judo, scouting (men versed in woodcraft were especially important), mountaineering, seamanship, engineering (demolitions and pioneer work), railway engine familiarization, weapons, knowledge of power plants, radio stations, communication and transportation centers."[21]

Screening for the first Ranger unit began in early June of 1942.

British Commando Monument in Scotland
Lou Lisko's Collection, United States
Army Military History Institute

—4—

Notes to Chapter 1

[1]. Eric Partridge, *Origins: A Short Etymological Dictionary of Modern English* (New York, New York: MacMillan, 1963), 549.

[2]. John K. Mahon, "Anglo-American Methods of Indian Warfare," *Mississippi Valley Historical Review*, 45, 1958, 254-275.

[3]. Edward S. Farrow, *A Dictionary of Military Terms* (New York, New York: Crowell Publishers, 1918), 490.

[4]. John R. Cuneo, *Robert Rogers of the Rangers* (New York, New York: Oxford University Press, 1959), 21, 28, 30-33.

[5]. Robert Rogers died in 1795. *Ibid.*, 33-35, 41-45, 52, 60-61. See also, David W. Hogan, Jr.'s dissertation, "The Evolution of the Concept of the U.S. Army's Rangers," 22-23, Duke University, 1986.

[6]. Center of Military History, "American Rangers from the Colonial Era to the Present," October 1, 1984, in "Rangers—General." See also Hogan, 25.

[7]. Walter Webb, *The Texas Rangers,* 2nd ed. (Boston, Massachusetts: Houghton Mifflin Co., 1965). See also Hogan 30.

[8]. John S. Mosby, *Mosby's War Reminiscence* (New York, New York: Pageant Book Co, 1958). See also "American Rangers from the Colonial Era to the Present."

[9]. Jerome J. Haggerty, "A History of the Ranger Battalions In World War II," dissertation, Fordham University, New York, 1982, 59.

[10]. *Ibid.*, 62.

[11]. Winston Churchill, *Their Finest Hour* (Boston, Massachusetts: Houghton Mifflin Company, 1949), 247.

[12]. Haggerty, 66.

[13]. *Ibid.,* 68.

[14]. *Ibid.* See also "Combined Operations Pamphlets," September 1942.

[15]. *Ibid.,* 70.

[16]. "Hard-Hitting Commandos," *New York Times Magazine*, April 5, 1942, 6.

[17]. Bruce Thomas, "The Commando," *Harper's Magazine*, March 1942, 438.

[18]. Lt. Gen. Lucian K. Truscott, Jr., *Command Missions: A Personal Story* (New York, New York: E. P. Dutton and Co., 1954), 22-23, 37.

[19]. *Ibid.,* 38.

[20]. Haggerty, 79-80.

[21]. *Ibid.*, 80.

Chapter 2

""Those Bastards Tried to Kill Us."
The 1st Ranger Battalion

Once the decision was made to establish a commando unit a competent leader was needed to organize and train them. William Darby, a native of Arkansas, had graduated from West Point in 1933 and joined the field of artillery. Throughout a period of eight years he served in various assignments, taking classes and gathering troop leadership experience. After Pearl Harbor, Darby was assigned to Maj. Gen. Russell P. Hartle, commander of the U.S. forces in Northern Ireland. As soon as Truscott had been authorized to create an elite force he directed Hartle to see to it.[1]

With little battle action at his present assignment, Darby asked a senior officer, Maj. Gen. Edmond H. Leavey, for a transfer. As Hartle spoke with Leavey about locating good leaders for this special unit, Leavey suggested William Darby.[2] The two generals went to Truscott with their recommendation, and thirty-one year old Darby was chosen as the 1st Ranger Battalion's commander.

Darby was a born leader, a characteristic true of all Rangers, officers and non-coms alike. As Marshall had stated in the beginning, officers must possess "leadership qualities of the highest order with special emphasis on initiative, judgment and common-sense."[3]

The call for volunteers immediately went out. An article in the *Saturday Evening Post* described the selection of recruits.

> To Darby's call, more than 2,000 men answered from more than fifty different Army units. The volunteers were promptly given stiff physicals and psychological tests, and then they were examined by Darby himself. The men he selected came from all states and professions. The youngest was PFC Lemuel Harris, eighteen years old, from Pocahontas, Virginia; the oldest was thirty-five year old Sergeant J. B. Commer, of Amarillo, Texas. There were Sergeant Dave Campbell, cabinetmaker; Captain Joe Fineberg, treasurer of a burlesque theater; Sergeant George Creed, coal miner from West Virginia, and T/5 Sampson P. Oneskunk, a full-blooded Indian from Cherry Creek, South Dakota. There were photographers, poets and Golden Gloves champions, a bullfighter, a cowboy and a church deacon.
>
> Of the 2,000 volunteers, 700 were selected and training began. Under Darby's direction, they were put through a seven-week Commando course in thirty-one days, with British Commandos as instructors.
>
> When training was done, only 520 of the original 700 still wanted to be Rangers and were still acceptable.[4]

Formal training of the 520 survivors of the initial screening began at Achnacarry, Scotland, the site of the British Commando Training Camp, and the 1st Ranger Battalion was born. The Battalion consisted of a Battalion Headquarters, a

Headquarters Company and six line companies.

In order to perform difficult and specialized missions the men had to be conditioned both in body and mind. Around the Commando Depot man-made obstacles such as high walls, ladders, ditches, and hedges created a grueling course. Lt. Col. William Darby continued with a description of their training.

> …The physical training course…was strenuous but well within our capabilities. We marched swiftly, swam rivers or crossed them on bridges made of toggle ropes…There were cliffs to climb, slides to tumble down, and when all that was quite enough, we played hard games.
>
> Borrowing from some of the ancient Scottish games, log exercises became ritual in our training. A group of men carrying a six-inch log on their shoulders tossed it about in an attempt to keep it off the ground.
>
> There was boxing and close-in-fighting. There was no particular emphasis on jujitsu, though the men were given a few good usable holds that each could be expected to remember and utilize when needed.
>
> Famous, and cursed by the Rangers, were the speed marches at the Commando Depot. Starting out with three-mile hikes, the training worked up to courses of five-, seven-, ten-, twelve-, and sixteen speed marches. On these we had to average better than four miles an hour over varied terrain, carrying full equipment. As we progressed in our physical training, we were sent on longer speed marches.[5]

The extensive hikes provided the maximum development to the soldier's lungs, legs and most importantly, his feet. They also revealed the character and perseverance of these volunteers. At the start the men suffered from blisters. Their feet were soon conditioned and became hard and tough. During one speed march Darby's Rangers hustled across ten miles in 87 minutes. To keep the men going in F Company, Lieutenant Cowerson would bellow out, "It is all in the mind and in the heart!" Tempted to drop out and rest on the soft green grass the Rangers thought twice about it. To fall out meant failure and returning to their old outfit in ignominy.[6]

In addition to the lengthy treks, the 1st Rangers endured three-day combat problems which climaxed with a mock battle. The Commandos believed that any trained soldier could march the first day over obstacles, up and down hills and through swamps. A competent trooper could even finish out a second day's course, but only a topnotch warrior could complete a third day of marching and still have strength enough to effectively fight. When the first three-day exercise concluded the 10% over-strength in Darby's unit had diminished to a 10% deficit.[7]

Not only was the physical conditioning more strenuous but also the instruction and practice in weaponry was more comprehensive than that received by the average World War II infantryman. Classes in firing all types of weapons, American and enemy, were conducted. They focused on field firing and the use of the bayonet at close quarters. At the Commando Depot the British erected a unique bullet and bayonet course. Here the men teamed up in pairs. While one soldier covered his buddy, the other climbed difficult obstacles such as a 14 foot wall. The trainee then had to leap, with his bayonet fixed, off the top to the muddy ground below. After both had successfully breached the wall, the pop-up targets tested their quick draw ability. The course ended with a quick hike up a steep slope while under fire. At the top the volunteers were expected to aggressively bayonet the targets.

The course also helped develop the individual soldier's initiative. Self-reliance and self-confidence became a large part of the Ranger character. They were required to do everything for themselves without waiting for an officer to relay orders. In battle the officer might not be there for his men; they were expected to survive and complete their mission on their own.

Overall, the exercises emphasized realism. Many times other commandos acted as the "enemy." They dressed in German uniforms, used their weapons and even spoke German. Commando snipers and machine-gunners would pepper the ground near the trainee. One Ranger frankly remarked, "Those bastards tried to kill us or we thought they did. We always maneuvered under live fire." It took only one close call and the Ranger would hug the ground henceforth. The course at Achnarry ended on August 1, 1942.[8]

Those that survived moved on to the Scottish Hebrides. Here their training involved a larger number of men and consisted mostly of amphibious landings. In mid-August, Lord Mountbatten invited Truscott to pick about 50 Rangers to participate in an upcoming raid on the German forces near Dieppe. Six officers and forty-four enlisted men were detached from the 1st Ranger Battalion. To gain the maximum experience forty were assigned to No. 3 Commando, six to No. 4, and the remainder to the Canadian unit.

On the morning of August 19, the men set out on their mission. From the start the No. 3 Commando unit was in trouble. German E-boats encountered the flotilla and foiled their surprise attack. Only a few boats reached the shore, and they met heavy fire from the enemy. The small commando unit suffered heavy losses, and the best they could do was to harass a German battery with sniper fire. The majority of commandos found themselves pinned down by rifle fire from houses and artillery fire from the cliffs. Only one squad out of the 5,000-man invasion could claim any achievements.

Six Rangers accompanied No. 4 Commando. The men landed and breached a wall and its surrounding barbed wire and headed for their objective - a German gun battery. They swiftly advanced inland, firing on the run. The Rangers entered and secured several farmhouses. Cpl. Franklin Koons found a good spot for sniping. He sighted an enemy soldier and pulled the trigger. It was one of the first kills by an American soldier. Mortars and shells soon plastered the adversary's artillery battery. One lucky shot landed in the battery's magazine, and British fighter planes came in on a low-level attack. The German guns were annihilated. By 11:00 a.m. the assailants safely withdrew.[9]

Although No. 4 Commando accomplished their mission, casualties were high; out of 5,000 men 3,400 were counted as killed or wounded. The Germans captured 1,000 soldiers that day. Among the American Rangers, 7 were killed or missing and 7 were wounded.[10]

The Liberation of Pointe du Hoc

* * * *

Despite the expedition's high casualty numbers and only partial success, the American people seemed to support the elite unit. Word of the Rangers' participation in the Dieppe raid soon spread, and the U.S. media awaited their chance to interview the combat-experienced 1st Rangers. All the major newspapers and magazines ran stories featuring this hand-picked American military team. *Newsweek* published an article describing the strenuous training. In New York, the newspapers ran headlines stating, "U.S. and Britain invade France," "U.S. Troops Land with Commandos in the Biggest Raid!" and "Tanks and U.S. Troops Smash at the French Coast!"[11]

Once the media attention had diminished, and the participants returned to their battalion, the unit traveled to Dundee, Scotland and conducted joint training with British No. 1 Commando unit. They learned methods of attacking pillboxes, batteries, and coastal defenses.[12] The Rangers were also trained in street fighting.

After Dieppe, the Allied Commanders felt the Rangers and Commandos could also be used in juxtaposition with infantry units in a large scale operation. Consequently, the 1st Ranger Battalion joined a composite of British-American Commandos known as the 1st and 6th "Commandies."[13] In addition, the U.S. generals saw the potential success for other Ranger units and in the summer of 1942 the 1st Special Service Force was established.

The American general's goal was to allow the 1st Rangers to gain more battle experience so that they could train forthcoming units. On September 24, 1942 Darby's battalion was assigned to the II Army Corps and finally attached to the 1st Infantry Division. Approximately one month later, October 26, the men embarked for North Africa.[14]

* * * *

On November 2, the officers divulged the plans for the 1st Rangers' first battle. Their objective was a four-gun battery on a high bluff near the port town of Arzew in Algiers. French troops, who sympathized with the Nazi regime (Vichy) defended the harbor and hamlet. The Americans soldiers were not enthusiastic about killing Frenchmen, and hoped that with great speed and surprise they would be able to capture the guns with little loss of life to both sides. On November 8, the assault on Arzew commenced. The mission proceeded like clock-work and was a complete success. Darby's Rangers felt cocky and realized all the hard and tedious training had paid off.[15]

Two months later, February, 1943, Darby's Rangers took on their next assignment. They were to give the impression that Allied strength in central Tunisia was much larger than was the case. To accomplish this feat the 1st Rangers conducted dangerous night raids, fast hit-and-run assaults and a heavy firing of weapons. Lieutenant Colonel Darby detailed the mission.

> The Rangers were to campaign behind...[the German line].
> In some ways we became a miniature Stonewall Jackson force,
> operating like the Confederate 'foot cavalry' in the Shenandoah

Valley during our Civil War.

A series of three raids was planned: one against an enemy position five miles northwest of Sened Station, another against Djebel el Ank, and a third against Medilla.[16]

On February 11 Darby, with a small squad, headed toward Sened Station. Allied trucks transported the group the first twenty miles. At a small French outpost they jumped out and commenced their march toward the enemy position. They traversed over very rugged terrain, but were able to quickly and quietly surprise the Italian soldiers manning the camp. In a heroic forced march, Darby's exhausted Rangers arrived back at the French outpost and hid out for a day. The U.S. high command dubbed the raid a success: 50 enemy soldiers dead, many others wounded, and 11 Italians from the 10th Bersaglieri Regiment were captured. The Italians dubbed the Rangers "Black Death." For his leadership and bravery the Army awarded William Darby the Silver Medal.[17] Ranger James Altieri reflected on the Sened Station mission.

> From now on there would be no illusions about what the future held for the Rangers and what would be expected of each man who wished to remain with them. The personal price was high, but so were the compensations - the self-satisfaction that one could keep up with the best in the Army, the knowledge that Ranger tactics were one of the most effective ways to defeat the enemy, shorten the war and save lives; the exhilarating camaraderie that comes only to soldiers who believe in their leaders and believe in the men they are fighting with.[18]

From Sened Station the 1st Battalion was to begin its raid against Djebel el Ank, but Army commanders countermanded this move and ordered all troops to leave the Gafsa area. The 1st Rangers' next assignment found them defending the Dernaia Pass on February 17. As the German divisions smashed the 1st Infantry Division at Kasserine Pass, Darby's men, except for one company which reinforced the 1st Division, sat quietly at Dernaia Pass. Lieutenant Colonel Darby did, however, send night patrols out. They ambushed Germans whenever possible and gained valuable night-time survival experience.

By March of '43 the 1st Ranger Battalion was fully experienced in combat, both on the large and small scale. U.S. commanders felt that many of the men would now be more useful training newly-formed Ranger units. On March 27, a handful of 1st Rangers were withdrawn from active combat duty; a few of the veterans were sent to the 2d Ranger Battalion and the 5th Ranger Battalion in order to help those units train for their significant and subsequent missions.[19]

The Liberation of Pointe du Hoc

Speed marches were an essential part of the Ranger conditioning. Harder routes were many times chosen in order to train the men to traverse over rough terrain during a battle and thus hit the enemy from an unlikely direction. James Altieri Coll., USAMHI

1st Rangers conduct amphibious training while being bombarded with live mortar shells. James Altieri Coll., USAMHI

Rangers crossing bridge by toggle rope.
James Altieri Coll., USAMHI

Members of the 1st Rangers climb and leap from a 14 foot barrier which was part of the course at
the Commando Depot, Achnacarry, Scotland.
James Altieri Coll., USAMHI

The Liberation of Pointe du Hoc

Rangers crossing a river by toggle rope while commandos fire live mortar shells at them. The courses stressed realism in their training.
James Altieri Coll., USAMHI

1ˢᵗ Rangers doing sit-ups while holding a log.
James Altieri Coll., USAMHI

Notes to Chapter 2

1   Dissertation by David W. Hogan, Jr., "The Evolution of the Concept of the U.S. Army Rangers, 1942-1983" (North Carolina: Duke University, 1986), 81-84.
2   Michael J. King, *William Orlando Darby: A Military Biography* (Hamden, Connecticut: Archon Books, 1981), 32.
3   Haggerty, 84.
4   Milton Lehman, "The Rangers Fought Ahead of Everybody," *The Saturday Evening Post,* June 15, 1946, 28-29.
5   William O. Darby and William H. Baumer, *Darby's Rangers: We Led The Way* (San Rafael, California: Presidio Press, 1980), 30-31.
6   James Altieri, *The Spearheaders* (New York, NY: The Bobb's-Merrill Co., Inc., 1960), 50-51.
7   Darby, 31.
8   *Ibid.,* 33 and 36.
9   *Ibid.,* 42-45.
10 *Ibid.,* 64-65.
11 *Ibid.*
12 Hogan, 62.
13 *Ibid.,* 69.
14 Darby, 49-50.
15 Altieri, 119-132.
16 Darby, 56.
17 *Ibid.,* 59.
18 Altieri, 223.
19 Lane, 13. The 1ˢᵗ Ranger Battalion continued to fight in Sicily and Italy.

Chapter 3

"What Kind of Nuts Were These Rangers?:"
Organizing and Training, 2d Ranger Battalion,
March 1943-May 1944

Army commanders had initially recommended the formation of the 2d Ranger Battalion back in December, 1942. Politicians in Washington, D.C., however, did not approve their organization until March, 1943, when hundreds of volunteers from various U.S. units arrived at the new Ranger school at Camp Forrest, Tennessee.

On March 29, 1943, the eager recruits gathered in a dusty field at Camp Forrest. The intense training began soon after. Every exercise and physical endurance test which the 1st Rangers had overcome was now inflicted on the rookies. Newcomers were given a canvas cot and blankets and sent to temporary barracks. The area soon came to be called Tent City. Colonel Becker, 11th Service Command, 2d Army, was acting commander of the battalion, and he felt that the men should live in combat conditions.[1]

The camp of the 2d Rangers looked atrocious. Streets turned muddy; the supply officer was forced to set up shop in an old, run down barn. Showers and baths had to be taken at a camp 1/2 mile away. And, although the food was at double rations, it was horrible.

If the conditions didn't discourage the recruits, the army physicals weeded out more of the them. Minor faults disqualified many of the men, but those who survived the initial exercises and physicals were inducted into the 2d Ranger Battalion. On April 1, 1943, the unit was officially activated.[2]

* * * *

SUBJECT: Activation of 2nd Ranger Battalion
AG 322.171-1 (GNMBF)   1st Ind.
(3-11-43)

HEADQUARTERS SECOND ARMY, Memphis, Tennessee.

TO: Commanding Officer, 11th Detachment Special Troops, Second Army Camp Forrest, Tennessee.

1. For compliance with applicable provisions of basic communication as amended.

2. Unit will be housed in tents in bivouac area.

3. You are directed to:
   (a) Issue the necessary Letter Orders activating the 2nd Ranger Battalion on April 1, 1943
   (b) Observe the transfer of personnel and equipment to this Battalion.
   (c) Assist the Commanding Officer, 2nd Ranger Battalion in obtaining

necessary supplies through Director of Supplies, Camp Forrest, Tennessee.

(d) Report observations and completion of activation to Headquarters Second Army.

4. Two copies activation directive as amended, Army Ground Forces enclosed.

- By command of Lieutenant General Lear:

LAWTON BUTLER,
Lt. Col., A.G.D.
Asst. Adjutant General[3]

* * * *

On April 15, Maj. L. E. McDonald assumed command of the Ranger Battalion and began organizing it. The 2d was arranged like the 1st Rangers. About 27 officers and 484 enlisted men comprised the unit. Headquarters and Headquarters Company had 9 officers and 94 enlisted men. Six line companies had 3 officers and 65 soldiers in each. The volunteers of the 2d Ranger Battalion hailed from all over the United States. Virtually every branch of service was represented: paratroopers, tankers, airmen, cooks, military police, intelligence, demolition experts and infantrymen.[4]

Those men who survived the first round of training felt cocky, but they soon learned that the first few weeks had not been that rough. By the second week of April the going got a lot tougher. The daily routine at Camp Forrest was as follows:

•6:00 a.m.: Drill Call! Awake, they ate and cleaned their tent area.

•Next was the Log Drill. This drill included an instructor yelling out, "Assume Position!" Five or six Rangers stepped up to a 14 foot log a foot in diameter. The officer then ordered, "Ready, Exercise!" Soldiers then lifted the log waist high. The instructor directed the men to raise the log over their heads, onto their right shoulders, and back down to their waist. This Log Drill lasted about 30 minutes.

•9:00 a.m.: The Rangers double-timed to a saw-dust pit. Two platoons, officers included, climbed into a saw-dust pit about 18 feet square. The pit had a waist high log barricade on all four sides. When the order to "Go" was given the soldiers from another group jumped in and attempted to throw the occupying Rangers out of the pit. It was anything goes, a total free-for-all. Men suffered from black eyes, broken feet, and sore knuckles.

•10:00 a.m.: After the brawl the Rangers double-timed to the obstacle course and sprinted through it. Carefully placed explosives sounded periodically with a violent burst.

•At 10:30 a.m.: it was speed marching, the walk-run kind. Many Rangers had athletes' foot and blisters.

•12:00 noon: Lunch, it was not a wonderful home-cooked dinner of steak, mashed potatoes and homemade bread, but it was an all-you-can-eat array of Army C-Rations: hash, carrots, canned peaches, bread, and watered-down coffee.

•1:00 p.m.: They were back to work with more drill running, crawling and hitting the dirt.

•3:30 p.m.: The men underwent demolition training. They sat for an hour listening carefully.

•4:30 p.m.: They double-timed back to Tent City and collapsed in their filthy living conditions.[5]

Each morning records were taken down of those men who dropped out and were returning to their original units. No shame was attached. This type of training was meant to carry a man to his limits and beyond. The Rangers would be asked to do the impossible in battle, and their bodies and spirits had to be in top condition.

While some were transferring out of the battalion in those three months, one was destined to join them. He received his orders to assume command of the 2d Rangers on June 30, 1943; his name was Maj. James Earl Rudder.

* * * *

James Earl Rudder, "Big Jim," was born in Eden, Texas, May 6, 1910; he was one of six sons. His father farmed and operated a livestock firm. When James graduated from Texas A & M in 1932 he was commissioned a second lieutenant in the Army Reserves. In 1933 he took a teaching and football coaching position at Brady High School. While there he met Margaret Williamson, a 1936 graduate of the University of Texas; they were married one year later. When war was declared the Army ordered him to active duty, and he attended the Infantry School at Fort Benning, Georgia. Rudder then served as a battalion executive officer at Camp Atterbury, Indiana. In the fall of '42 he went to the Army Command and General Staff College.[6] Arriving at Camp Forrest, Tennessee, Maj. James Rudder immediately began making his battalion into a better, more effective fighting unit.

James Earl Rudder at Pointe du Hoc. Lisko Ranger Box, USAMHI

The Liberation of Pointe du Hoc

When Rudder arrived at Tent City he was appalled at the horrible living conditions, and he moved the battalion into wooden barracks with indoor latrines and showers. But better living conditions were not the only changes to be established. Rudder also initiated a monthly gripe session. One of the first complaints was about the atrocious food they had been forced to eat for the past few months. Major Rudder sent the battalion cooks to school. When the food did not improve, the commander sent the cooks back to school.

Throughout the summer months the Rangers continued their rigorous physical training. During one exercise the battalion was ordered to make a 36 mile hike in 12 hours surviving on one canteen of water. It was a drill which the 1st Rangers had had to perform in Scotland. The one element the high command forgot, however, was that Scotland and Tennessee summers are quite different. The humidity in Tennessee was quite oppressive. T/5[7] Herman Stein, a member of D Company at the time, recalled this specific training exercise:

> ...By mid-afternoon the fellows were dropping out like flies and Slater [D Company's commander at the time] was becoming pretty exhausted himself. One thing he had guts and he'd stay marching till he fell. This happened eventually due to an attack of stomach cramps. A few of us including Pat McCrone, Snake Johnson, and myself held a little critique of our own and decided — if these guys want to run themselves into exhaustion go ahead, but we're going to do something about it. On one extended break we stopped by a swampy section, filled up our canteens, added a couple of iodine pills and presto — instant revitalization. This was the civilian's soldier's way of thinking — you take orders to a degree but when it interferes with your rationalization, and you start performing like a zombie, then it's time to do something about it. Many times under fire we made up our own minds what to do.[8]

The intense and unrelenting training caused many men to drop out, but other eager soldiers transferred in. The battalion remained in Tennessee until early September 1943.

* * * *

On September 4, '43 the whole 2d Ranger battalion packed their bags and headed for the Scouts and Raiders School at Fort Pierce, Florida. After several tedious days of delay, due to the shortage of transportation, the men boarded their locomotive and headed for sunny Florida. The ride consisted of reading and card playing. T/5 Francis "Killer" Kolodziejczak, of HQ Company, cleaned up, and after a long, hot journey the 2d Rangers disembarked at Fort Pierce.

The infantrymen noted that the Scouts and Raiders School accommodated mostly sailors who, at this time, were nicknamed "Frogmen" because they trained in amphibious exercises, and it was here that the Rangers began preparing for the Normandy invasion.[9] The course was crammed into 11 days and focused on training in rubber boats and LCA craft. In addition to the physical training, classroom courses were taught by sailors who had participated in the invasions of Tunisia and Sicily.[10] Members from HQ Company described the intense exercises.

> The course was centered about rubber boats and LCAs…The first day was to look over the boats, learn how to blow them up, patch 'em and to gain confidence in this over stuffed waffle.
>
> Next day we took a trip around the jetty to another beach. It was here that many had their first failure, finding the undertow and incoming tide made it almost impossible to launch the boats in the surf and had to return the easy, short way; getting "raspberried" from those who had conquered "Father Neptune."
>
> Non-swimmers gained confidence in their "Mae Wests" which held up any "Floundering Fauntleroy" not acquainted with the

Cpl. Lou Lisko, HQ Company, 2d Rangers operating Signal Corps radio (SCR 284) mounted on a jeep, Camp Forrest, Tennessee, 1943. Lisko Ranger Box, USAMHI

ability to coordinate movement of arms, feet and lungs to advantage.

A sequence of training events included landing on rock jetties, loading and unloading into LCAs from landing nets, going out off-shore and studying silhouettes in the evening; company and Battalion cross-country marches which included portage of boats, making a beach head, infiltrating through beach-sentries, attacking small installations, sending beach marking teams ashore who landed prior to H-hour, first slitting their boats in the breakers and crawling to the dune-line after which they sent signals of colored lights, made directional by means of hand-made hoods. Boat teams paddled around the island to gain coordination and finally the attack on Fort Pierce itself.[11]

Amazingly only one man in HQ Company fell victim to the rocks during the dangerous exercises. S/Sgt. James K. Patrick, Jr., received a cracked rib while making a jetty landing. Other Rangers, however, became casualties when their boats sank, and they plunged into the deceptively beautiful, cool, serene ocean. While trying to reach shore, numerous jelly fish would assault them, leaving nasty sting marks over their entire body.

Not only was the amphibious training intense, but the Rangers found themselves in an all-out battle with the bugs: gnats, huge mosquitoes, and sand flies. The flying pests infiltrated their food and tried to draw every last drop of blood and sanity from these brawny lads. To cope with the cruel, unforgiving environment and exercises, Pvt. Paul French and Fleming, both from HQ Company, supplied the battalion non-coms with fire water. In many tents one could find, buried under the sand in their shelters, empty bottles of liquor. The alcohol boosted the men's spirits after a long day of grueling maneuvers, but the two privates' little scheme was discovered, and the officers promptly placed them on "trash detail" - a smelly, despised duty.

Besides the hooch, the Rangers enjoyed eating the local coconuts. Headquarters' boys coaxed Pvt. Vincent W. Malisa to climb a palm tree and throw down the tasty fruit. The unit's kitchen was at an all-time low, and the men needed to find nutrition any way they could. In many cases the Navy allowed the men to obtain a good cup of coffee and a sandwich or two at their mess hall.

After the tenth day, the Rangers had had enough of sunny Florida. But they still had to endure their last exercise. It would be their toughest night and consisted of a grand, mock assault on the local town. The attack was made on Fort Pierce and its airport. Though the commandos startled many citizens, no one was injured and the exercise was dubbed a success. Overall the school was excellent, and the men were in better shape than ever.[12]

After many days of confinement to camp the men obtained passes to town. At the bars it seemed there was always someone willing to challenge a Ranger to see how tough these guys really were. At one of the saloons a sailor began taunting Sgt. Charles Kettering, D Company. Like many soldiers, Kettering was eager to defend his honor and gave the man a good beating.[13] T/4[14] William Weber, HQ Company, recalled that "...everyone went hog-wild, doing anything and everything; causing the Naval School commander no end of grief and forcing our restriction to the area for our last evening in "Sunny Florida.""[15]

Left to right: Louis Herman, Stive and Lou Lisko hanging out at Fort Pierce, Florida
Lisko Ranger Box, USAMHI

* * * *

After spending 11 days at Fort Pierce, the Rangers relocated to Fort Dix, New Jersey on September 14, 1943. Most of the men of the 2d Battalion hailed from New York, New Jersey and Pennsylvania. They hoped to receive furloughs and be able to see their families and friends. But first the boys had to get organized and oriented to their new surroundings and to the new program.

With their initial amphibious training behind them, the exercises at Fort Dix focused on range firing, section, company and battalion coordination problems, artillery demonstrations and a two-day operation by companies with prepared objectives to attack and annihilate. Strenuous calisthenics and marches rounded out their tight schedule.

The non-stop rigors of drilling and marching took a toll on many of the men. A few could not resist the temptations brought on by their close proximity to home. Private Fleming, HQ Company, yearned to see his girlfriend in Pennsylvania. The private didn't think the Army would miss a 2 1/2 ton truck so he borrowed one and took off. He didn't stop until an axle broke while on the Pennsylvania turnpike. T/5 William Clark, Jr., HQ Company, also mysteriously disappeared. After two days of being AWOL (absent without leave) he showed up. He provided a tale of being extremely sick with the "flu." But his buddies felt they knew better and said, "Clark 'flu the coop,'" and "It was a straight case of the DTs."[16]

Their stay at Fort Dix was briefly interrupted on October 21 when orders came down to load up the trucks and head for Camp Richie, Maryland, for two days of intelligence training. They embarked at 4:00 a.m. and arrived in Maryland about 5:30 p.m. the next day. William Weber, HQ Company, explained their training there:

the problem...was to take high ground, held by troops in

German uniforms and using Boche weapons [and speaking German]. The exercise went very well for the following morning we actually reached our objective and were declared the winners, receiving high praise from the school heads. At its completion we had a demonstration of enemy weapons, mine fields, booby traps and tactics.[17]

By October 23 the Rangers returned to Fort Dix and resumed their tactical firing training and physical conditioning. It was at this time that they endured one of their toughest hikes in their military careers. They scaled oil piles some 50 feet high, ran cross-country, scrambled through brush, and crawled through sewer pipes. The lads were completely exhausted and smelled of sewage and sweat.

Notwithstanding the few negative memories of Fort Dix, the men also recalled many good times at the camp. One of the highlights was when the proud band of Rangers donned their dress uniforms and lined up by company to pose for their unit photographs. They smiled for the birdie, but quietly wondered to themselves how many would be able to assemble for the next full unit photo-shoot. For the survivors, these photographs would become cherished mementos. A tear can be seen in the old veteran's eyes as he peers at the faces of his fallen comrades, the ones who never made it home. With their pictures captured for posterity, the men held a farewell bash in Trenton on November 10.

* * * *

The next day they left New Jersey by train and started north. They then caught a ferry and crossed into Camp Shanks, New York. Rudder's Rangers crammed into long, narrow hutments with two small stoves to combat the chilly November weather. Word trickled down that they were to be shipped out any day. They nervously checked and packed their equipment. The medics administered last minute tetanus shots. Finally, after several months of challenging training, the battalion boarded the *Queen Elizabeth* on November 21, 1943, and headed for the European Theatre of Operations.[18]

On December 1 the 2d Ranger Battalion arrived at Grenach, Scotland.[19] They then proceeded to Bude, England which became their home base. Once at Bude the men continued their amphibious training in the Atlantic Ocean and began scaling the high and rocky cliffs along the west coast — moving ever closer to their destiny and the Pointe-du-Hoc mission.

The Rangers now learned from and practiced with the renowned British commandos. By late December a detachment of 2d Rangers moved to a small village called Titchfield on the southern coast of England. The men were housed in private homes in the surrounding area.

Just before New Year's Eve rumors circulated that some of the battalion were going to see action. Another 94 hand-picked Rangers from Company A were sent to Folkestone. There, they learned that they would be sent to Calais, France. With the help of several French guides, they were to capture a German soldier — any soldier, to interrogate concerning their forces situated on the coast of France.

* * * *

The commanders formulated two plans and split the detachment into four teams. Boarding LCIs (larger than the LCAs) at Dover, they would secretly move across the English Channel and anchor several miles off shore. They would then board LCAs and land in France. If all went well in plan A, they would capture a German on the beach, recall the LCAs, and head back to England. If plan A did not work, plan B would be initiated. The four groups of Rangers were given distinct missions.

Group One was ordered to cut the beach wire, clear a section through the mine field, and set up a perimeter to cover the beach exit. Group Two was directed to quietly weave their way through the barbed wire. If discovered, they were to blow a hole through the wire, search, clear and secure the area. The other two groups would cover the second group's operation.[20] Since the operation's success lay in part in landing in complete darkness only three nights in January, 1944, would be dark enough to allow the men complete cover. When each of these three successive nights arrived the Royal Navy, which had been directed to transport the Americans, postponed the raid.

On January 27, the entire mission was canceled; the Company A boys were extremely disappointed. They had worked hard to prepare for this raid. Ultimately it was deemed too risky. The Navy could have dropped the Rangers at the beach, but it would have been impossible to remain off the coast of France in the tumultuous channel to await their return.

> Several Rangers from Company D went through a similar experience. Approximately 15 men were picked to reconnoiter the Isle of Herm. The men from D Company trained with the Fourth British Commando Group and gained valuable lessons, but they were discouraged to hear that their mission had also been recalled.

* * * *

After both raids had been quashed Companies A and D reunited with the battalion, and they moved to Warsesh and stayed with the local English residents. While the 2d Rangers had not seen combat action as yet, many men were injured during the numerous and difficult training exercises. T/4 Owen L. Brown, Communications Section, Headquarters Company recalled his accident on February 11:

> ... We were ordered to take down the wire lines between Warsesh, Tidsfield, and prepare for a move. [Working all day at about]...3:30 p.m., George Clarke asked if we would be done in time for him to catch the 4:30 bus, as he had a date with a Danish nurse. George and I were roommates so I tried to help him keep his date. At 4:10 p.m. with 4 pulls to go, I found I could not throw the combat wire we were using out over the street lamp below me. The street lamp pole was about 5 feet closer to the street than the utility pole I was on. About 12 feet in the air, the street lamp had a cross arm, and from there, it was arched out over the street. I

The Liberation of Pointe du Hoc

1st Platoon, Company F, Fort Dix, New Jersey, 1943. Front and to right: Lt. Jacob Hill
Gene Elder Coll.

1st Platoon, Company F, Fort Dix, New Jersey, 1943
Front Row, from right: Sgt. Charles Frederick, Capt. Otto Masny
Gene Elder Collection, names provided by Herman Stein

decided I could jump from the wood pole to the cross arm and drop the wire over the lamp then slide down the middle of the lamp pole and proceed with the job. I jumped with my spurs on and landed on the cross arm and caught the arch of the lamp. I believe it was cast iron because it snapped off, and I fell backward with the arch part of the lamp coming on top of me and hitting me in the chest, chin, and forehead. I was totally paralyzed but conscious…Lou Herman was the first on to me, and he put his hands over his face, and said, 'My God, he's dead,' and ran away from me. Then George Clarke came up, took charge. He sent someone to the motor pool at Lord Mountbatten's summer home, about 3 blocks down the street for an ambulance. The men put me in the ambulance, and George Clarke went with me to the hospital, ignoring the date we were rushing for him to keep…This hospital was a British military hospital…being in transition, it was short-staffed, and most patients were British. They took me off the stretcher and put me on a bed. I could hear the men around me talking. I was replacing another ranger who had fallen from a cliff and was in the hospital for observation, and now I come in after my fall, and they were wondering what kind of nuts these rangers were.[21]

The doctors x-rayed Brown and told him he looked terrible. His arm was broken, and he was bruised all over. On the third day of his hospitalization, Brown "borrowed" a British overcoat and put it over his hospital pajamas. He then donned a hat and put his G.I. shoes on and made a quick get away. T/4 Brown headed for Warsesh. He wandered all night and safely returned to the house where he had been staying.

In the morning Brown cleaned himself up and headed for Tidsfield. Before he could enter the brick building being used as headquarters he met his captain, George S. Williams. Captain Williams immediately began reprimanding Brown and escorted him to a jeep. Williams ordered, "I don't want to see you until the doctors release you, or I'll come and get you." Owen Brown found himself back at the British hospital—that same day the doctors released him.[22]

Medical Section, HQ Company. Captain Block on right of frontline

Headquarters Company, Communications and I & O Section

Headquarters Company, Communications and I and O Section, Continued
Lt. James Eikner, front row, second from left.

Headquarters Company, Communications and I & O Section, continued

The Liberation of Pointe du Hoc

Headquarters
Second from left: Lt. Col. Rudder; Second from right: Capt. Walter Block

Headquarters
Second from right: Capt. Harold Slater

Notes to Chapter 3

[1] Lane, 18-19.

[2] Hogan, 203.

[3] George M. Clark, William Weber and Ronald Paradis, *2nd Ranger Battalion: The Narrative History of Headquarters Company, April 1943-May 1945*. Np, Nd, 20, Military History Institute, Carlisle Barracks, Carlisle, Pennsylvania.

[4] Lane, 18-19.

[5] *Ibid.*, 19-21.

[6] Haggerty, note 5, 203.

[7] T/5 = Technician 5th grade equivalent to a corporal. Both wore sleeve chevrons and two stripes. The technicians also had a T under the two stripes. A designation no longer used by the Army. The T-ranking identified service personnel: cooks, radio operators, etc., verified by James Eikner, Bob Slaughter and Bill Dean. Guido Rosignoli, *Army Badges and Insignia of World War II*, New York: MacMillan, 1972.

[8] Herman Stein's transcript supplied by Herman Stein on June 17, 1999.

[9] The "frogmen" would become known as the Navy Seals.

[10] Lane, 26-27.

[11] Lt. James Eikner, HQ Company, acted as fact editor for George M. Clark, William Weber and Ronald Paradis, *2nd Ranger Battalion,* 29-30.

[12] *Ibid.* See also Lane, 26-27.

[13] World War II Ranger and eyewitness Len Lomell, D Company, 2d Ranger Battalion. Notes to author, July 27, 1999.

[14] T/4 = Technician 4th grade equivalent to a buck sergeant. Both wore sleeve chevrons with three stripes, the technician having a T below the stripes. Again, this is a specialty rank. They conducted cook detail, acted as radio operators, but the T/4, though a sergeant, had no authority over corporals or privates. Verified by James Eikner, Bob Slaughter and Bill Dean, Rosignoli, *Army Badges*.

[15] Clark, 30.

[16] *Ibid.*, 32-33.

[17] *Ibid.*

[18] *Ibid.*, 35.

[19] Lane, 35-37.

[20] *Ibid.*, 47.

[21] Oral History Transcript by Owen L. Brown, HQ Company, 2d Ranger Battalion, the Eisenhower Center, New Orleans, Louisiana, 10-11.

[22] *Ibid.*, 12.

Chapter 4

" Lovely Cliffs…":
Preparing for the Invasion

Just one month prior to Brown's accident, Rudder, who had been promoted to lieutenant colonel, had received the 2d Ranger's mission for Overlord. A staff study conducted by the 21st Army Group concluded that the Rangers and Commandos could be used in independent tasks in support of the Overlord assault. Furthermore, they resolved that one of the most difficult and significant strategical objectives in the Invasion would be taking out the coastal defense battery at Pointe-du-Hoc.[1]

The German battery about four miles west of Omaha Beach held six huge 155mm captured French guns. With a range of 25,000 yards, or approximately 10 miles, they could easily enfilade Omaha Beach where the 1st and 29th Infantry Divisions would land. The German-held guns could also devastate Utah Beach where the 4th Infantry Division was expected. In point of fact, their range was extensive enough to prevent the troop ships in the Channel from coming in too close, giving the landing craft more distance to cover to deliver their cargo of men and weapons to the shore. To take out these guns the Allied commanders chose the three line companies — D, E and F — and elements from Communications and Intelligence & Operations of Headquarters Company, 2d Rangers, with attached Medics.

Pointe-du-Hoc seemed impregnable to the Axis generals. A strong defensive line of trenches, anti-aircraft guns, machine gun nests nestled in the cliff, protected the German battery. They built underground shelters and magazines made of reinforced concrete 3' to 6' 6" thick. The shelters, magazines, and gun emplacements were connected by trenches. Aerial and intelligence studies reported that the precise location of the huge guns were at grid coordinates 586937. The guns were on wheel mountings. The wheels were secured to a central pivot on a concrete emplacement about 40 feet in diameter. Netting helped camouflage each piece. No turrets or gun shields were provided, but a reinforced concrete observation post helped direct the gun fire.[2] To defend from a landward attack, the Germans circled the fortress with mines and wire. They also placed machine guns and anti-aircraft guns on their right and left flanks to protect their precious guns.

The least expected, and most difficult way to approach the guns, was from the sea. Not only would the Rangers have to traverse the rough English Channel in small landing craft, make it to shore through the hail of machine gun and rifle fire, they would have to scale an 83' to 100' cliff. Using ropes and ladders the men would climb the bluff while being fired upon by German defenders. If the Rangers survived that onslaught, they would then work their way through barbed wire, mine fields, and large underground bunkers made of reinforced concrete connected by underground tunnels. Each squad would be given a unique mission.

While Rudder understood the challenge of their mission, the Rangers themselves knew very little of their assigned Overlord tasks. Many of them were extremely bored and tired of all the special training with no resulting action. Lieutenant Colonel Rudder realized his most immediate enemy was low morale. Combined with the

The Liberation of Pointe du Hoc

A French 155mm gun captured by the Germans, probably not one of the guns at the Pointe.
The Germans used this gun in Libya.
Col. G. B. Jarrett Collection, USAMHI

Another example of a French 155mm cannon in a gun emplacement at the Pointe.

Aerial view of the Pointe looking south. Lisko Ranger box, USAMHI

A closer view of Pointe-du-Hoc from the west. Looking down on the eastern portion of the
Pointe. This is the beach where all the Ranger LCAs landed.
Lisko Ranger Box, USAMHI.

The Liberation of Pointe du Hoc

This is the area where Company D was supposed to land. Tourist are congregating near the Ranger monument at the Pointe. Lisko Ranger Box, USAMHI.

knowledge of their difficult task and with the goal of keeping the men busy, Rudder began in January, '44, to specifically train his men for the Invasion.

Rigorous hiking and speed marches, along with daily exercises, kept the Rangers focused on getting through the day, and not on their boredom. Squad, section and platoon firing training helped them to perfect their skills in the use of individual weapons. In addition, they learned the function of wire communications men and their equipment. T/4 Brown personally worked with each line company explaining to the Rangers the importance of the communication's men and why they should be protected.[3]

Lt. George Kerchner, Company D, recalled the strenuous preparation for D-Day:

> ...early in January we began this intensive training in climbing of cliffs and working in amphibious landing from assault landing craft. We moved around to various parts of England, I think they had scouts out trying to find the highest and most difficult cliffs that they could find...early in January [we] went to a little town outside of Portsmith called Park Gate...Most of our training while we [were] at Park Gate was working with these [British] landing craft that were manned by British sailors.[4]

In early February the battalion was transported by British LCAs (landing craft assault) to the Isle of Wight for two weeks of intensive training up the chalk cliffs. Lieutenant Kerchner remembered that there were

> ...lovely cliffs there to look at, on one side of the Isle they had these chalk cliffs that were two to two hundred fifty feet high, and we work[ed] on those most of the time and right around these cliffs that were called Pennisen [sic] cliffs...the tallest cliffs that we

worked on over in England…were about three hundred and fifty feet high.[5]

In mid-February the Rangers moved back to Bude, England and continued their cliff climbing training. Here they tried different techniques in scaling the heights. Sometimes they used ropes; at other times they experimented with four foot steel ladders which the soldier connected as he moved up the sheer rock face. A Ranger climbed to the top of the ladder and added an extension. It was an awkward and nerve-racking process; the individual was 100 feet in the air weighed down with heavy gear and weapons.[6]

While in Bude some of the men and officers were transferred out of the unit and new ones arrived to take their place. On March 4, the 2d added a cannon platoon consisting of four half-tracks mounting 75mm guns.[7] By the end of March, Lieutenant Colonel Rudder felt that his men had earned some time off, and he granted most of them five day passes. One company at a time could take five days off. Many men remained in Bude and slept.[8]

Revived in body and spirit, the battalion moved to the Assault Training Center at Braunton in April. The course lasted seven days. Here they rehearsed more amphibious assaults, fire and movement exercises, breaching beach wire, attacking fixed defensive positions, demolitions setting, handling shape charges, detecting and deactivating booby traps and street fighting. The men specifically worked on assaulting pillboxes and handling flamethrowers, bazookas, bangalore torpedoes, rifle grenades, and thermite grenades. Communication's personnel practiced using SCR 300 radios. Squads drilled and then reassembled for platoon and company-wide exercises.[9] All of this training was in direct correlation with the upcoming invasion.

A typical problem consisted of the men attacking an "enemy" position — usually at the top of a hill. Using live explosives to simulate combat noise and stress, the wire cutting team worked their way through the barbed wire. A rifle-squad would lay down protective fire. In the rear a bazooka team, flamethrower team, demolition men, and anti-tank soldiers spread out and advanced on the enemy pillboxes while laying down fire. Once the position had been taken, the groups quickly reorganized and prepared for a counterattack. This simulated a likely scenario for the Rangers on D-Day.

＊ ＊ ＊ ＊

On April 9, '44, Companies D, E and F and a selected number from Headquarters Company transferred to Swanage. Since these units were designated to take Pointe-du-Hoc they required additional instruction in scaling cliffs. The Rangers used rockets with ropes attached to them. Mounted on the LCAs the rockets were fired when the vessels reached the shore. The grappling hook would hopefully bite into the bomb-blasted earth on the Pointe, and the men would scramble up the ropes. A description of the special equipment developed for the landing was given:

Each of the 10 LCAs (landing craft assault boats, designed to carry approximately thirty-five soldiers) were fitted with 3 pairs of rocket guns, firing grapnels which pulled up (by pairs) 3/4 inch plain ropes, toggle ropes, and rope ladders. In addition, each craft carried a pair of small hand-projection-type rockets, which could be easily carried ashore and fired small ropes. Each craft also carried tubular-steel extension ladders made up of light four-foot sections suitable for quick assembly. Four DUKWS mounted a 100-foot extension ladder, fire department type. Personnel of the assault parties carried minimum loads, with heavier weapons amounting to four B.A.R.s [Browning Automatic Rifles] with two 60mm mortars per company. Two supply craft brought in packs, rations, demolitions, and extra ammunition for the three companies.[10]

Another interesting, experimental piece of equipment used was a 100 foot extension ladder on an amphibious DUKW. The DUKWs were 2 1/2 ton General Motors trucks with six wheel drive, a boat hull, rudder and propeller. In the water they could move slowly toward shore using the propeller and rudder. Once on shore the DUKW driver drove up the beach to extend a huge firemen's ladder. The Rangers could then quickly scale the cliff. Four extension ladders, borrowed from the London Fire Company, were placed on the DUKWs.[11]

* * * *

On April 27, 1944, the 2d Rangers reunited and the entire battalion, along with the 5th Ranger Battalion, participated in a joint exercise dubbed Fabius I. Elements of the 116th Infantry Regiment, 29th Infantry Division, were also conducting training in the same area as the two Ranger battalions.

The men boarded LSIs and headed out to sea. They had no way of knowing whether this was the real thing. They spent two relaxing days and nights on the ships. The soldiers welcomed rest from the rigorous training. On the third morning, the Rangers boarded the LCAs which were then lowered into the water with ropes.

At dawn the boats moved inland, and the Rangers stormed the beach and set up defenses to the right of the 29th Infantry Division. Companies D, E and F scaled a cliff and advanced inland; Company D led the way. The three companies reached Combe Point, their objective for the mission. They then began a long, 12 mile speed march with full combat gear to Little Dartmouth. They secured the area and set up a defensive position and awaited the other companies of the 2d Ranger Battalion.[12]

Up to this point the operation had gone unnoticed by German war planes or their Navy; however, on the fourth day German E-boats and bombers sighted the exercise. Bombs rained down on the 29th and Ranger battalions. In addition the German E-boats fired on the soldiers. T/4 Owen Brown, Communications, recalled the scene.

German E-boats managed to sneak in and shoot up our men and equipment. I was on the side of a hill stringing wire when bullets started bouncing off the ground around me. I dashed up the hill about 30 yards to a rope [near] a stone wall...There were a lot of casualties that day. Our first enemy fire, and so unexpected.[13]

LCA 722 during training exercises in England.   The rockets are pointed toward the cliff.
Lisko Ranger Box, USAMHI

Ropes being rocket-fired toward the cliffs in a practice run in England.
Lisko Ranger Box, USAMHI

Two DUKWs -- amphibious trucks -- coming to shore -- no extension ladders are shown. Photo taken August 15, '44, showing the 45th Division hitting southern France. These are not Ranger units in the photograph, USAMHI.

Notes to Chapter 4

1. Hogan, 160-161.
2. Lane, 72-73.
3. Brown, 13.
4. Oral History Transcript by George Kerchner, Co. D, 2d Ranger Battalion, the Eisenhower Center, New Orleans, Louisiana, 1.
5. Ibid., 1-2.
6. Lane, 55-56.
7. Hogan, 162.
8. Lane, 57.
9. Hogan, 162 and Weber, 51. The men from D, E, F Company and personnel from HQ Company did not take flamethrowers with them. They were too heavy and cumbersome.
10, Omaha Beachhead, 6 June-13 June 1944, Historical Division, War Department (Washington D.C.: U.S. Government Printing, 1945), 88.
11. Lane, 60-61.
12 Ibid., 63.
13 Brown, 13.

Chapter 5

"The Most Dangerous Mission of D-Day":
The Pointe-du-Hoc Assignment

Back in January of 1944, when Gen. Omar Bradley, commander of the First Army Group, had explained to Lt. Col. James Rudder the proposed Pointe-du-Hoc assignment, the general finished by saying, "It is the most dangerous mission of D-Day." Lieutenant Colonel Rudder looked at General Bradley and replied, "My Rangers can do the job."[1]

It was now five months after that significant discussion, and the two teamed battalions (2d and 5th Ranger Battalions) moved to Swanage and continued cliff-scaling training. In late May they were taken to their staging area near Dorchester and put under tight security. On June 1, 1944 Companies D, E, F and elements from Communications and Intelligence & Operations from Headquarters Company boarded their British transport, *HMS Ben Machree* and *Amsterdam*.[2] Companies A, B, C went on *HMS Prince Charles*. The officers now briefed them about the overall mission.

Allied Commanders had dubbed the Invasion "Overlord." A huge armada had been organized to participate in this assault. The Provisional Ranger Group was attached to the United States V Army Corps, whose task was to take the beachhead between Porten-Bessin and the Vire River on the coast of France.

The initial assault wave, "Force O," consisted of the 1st Infantry Division, the 29th Infantry Division, and the Provisional Ranger Force.[3] The 1st Infantry Division would land to the left of the 29th Infantry Division on Omaha Beach—sectors Fox Green, Fox Red and Easy Red. The 29th Infantry Division would also hit Omaha Beach in the sectors of Easy Green, Dog Red, Dog White and Dog Green (see map 2).

The Provisional Ranger Force was temporarily attached to the 116th Infantry Regiment, 29th Infantry Division. The commanders split the Ranger force into two sections: Task Force A and Task Force B. Companies D, E, F and selected men from Headquarters Company comprised Task Force A. At their H-Hour, 6:30 a.m., they would hit Pointe-du-Hoc, located about four miles from Omaha Beach. Company D would land on the west side, and Companies E and F would hit the east side of the Pointe. Each boat team had a specific job. When they climbed the sheer cliffs, they would take out the big gun emplacements and the other fortifications in the area. They were to then make their way inland, secure the black-top highway, and hold it until relieved: to prevent German reinforcements from reaching the beach areas and to kill or capture any enemy forces retreating. They were to cut German communications from the west side of Omaha Beach to Utah Beach. Once Rudder's men had safely climbed the cliffs, he would signal Task Force B, waiting in their LCAs close to the Pointe.

When Lt. Col. Max Schneider, commander of the 5th Ranger Battalion, and A and B Companies of the 2d Ranger Battalion, received the signal his men would land on the Pointe and join with Rudder's boys to push south toward the coastal highway, known to be the main German communications route to their defenses in the Grandcamp-Vierville area (see map 3). A strong defensive position was to be established just west on the black-top road until the 116th Infantry Regiment arrived from Vierville.[4]

The plan directed Force C, comprised of Company C, 2d Ranger Battalion, and an amphibious tank platoon, to land on Charlie Beach just to the right of Dog Green Sector, Omaha Beach. They were to destroy the installations at Pointe-El-Raz-de-La Perce. Once this was completed they would join Task Force A near the Pointe.[5]

If Schneider did not receive word from Rudder, Task Force B was to land at Dog Green sector, Omaha Beach. After getting to shore they were to move quickly through the 116th and make their way to Pointe-du-Hoc to link up with Rudder's men. The combined force would knock the Germans out of the Pointe and move west fighting their way to Grandcamp, their next objective

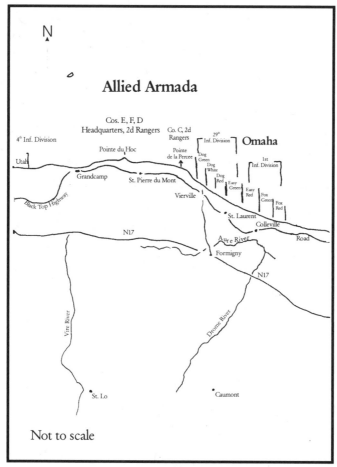

Map 2

Omaha Beach landing sectors, scheduled landings were to begin at 6:30 a.m. If Task Force B did not hear from Rudder Companies A and B, 2d Ranger Battalion and the 5th Ranger Battalion were to land at Dog Green sector.

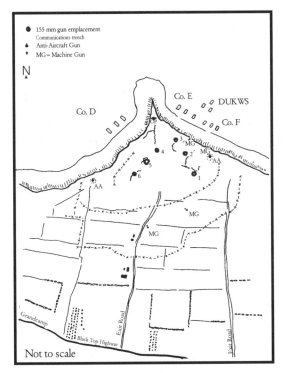

Map 3

Plan A: Comapny D, 2nd Rangers was to land on the west side of the Pointe; Companies E and F would hit the Pointe from the east. Once Rudder's task force succeeded he would radio back to the *Prince Charles* and Task force B would land at the Pointe.

✳   ✳   ✳   ✳

Intelligence reports indicated that the German unit opposing the Rangers on the six guns were the 2d Battery—832nd Army Coastal Battery. It was estimated that more than 200 artillery and infantrymen defended the Pointe. The infantrymen were from the 726th Infantry Regiment, 716th Infantry Division. Approximately 40% of the 716th were non-German and 75% of those were Polish. About 150 German artillerymen had been stationed near St. Pierre du Mont, and a reserve battalion was deployed at Bayeux. In addition, rumors had spread that the German general, Erwin Rommel, was dissatisfied with the Atlantic Wall defenses. If Rommel was displeased then the area must have a weakness.

To soften the area, the U.S. Eighth Army Air Command and British bombers hit the Pointe on May 22 and June 4. And, just prior to the landing on June 6, the Army Air Corps bombed the area again. Navy Ships then raked the area with their big guns at H-hour minus 20 minutes. Allied Commanders assumed that the intense bombing would take out most of the defenses. Those enemy soldiers who remained, a number of whom were conscript troops, would no doubt retreat or surrender. In addition, the Allies believed it would take the Germans at least an hour for their reserves to reach Omaha or Pointe-du-Hoc. By that time the Rangers from Task Force A would have secured the area. It would not be realized until much later that the Allied bombing had missed their mark by about 3 miles. The German forces on the Normandy coast were still intact on the morning of June 6.

Notes to Chapter 5

1. See James W. Eikner, "Rangers can do the job," The Houston Post, Tuesday, June 5, 1984, 3B, and Lou Lisko, "The Guns of Pointe du Hoc -- D-Day -- WWII -- Omaha Beach --Normandy, France -- June 6, 1944," handout provided by Len Lomell.
2. Cpl. Lou Lisko, HQ Company Testimony, in Sylvie Chapelie's "The American Example 'Overlord,'" 135, 2d Ranger Box 1, Photo Archives, United States Military History Institute, Carlisle Barracks, Carlisle, Pennsylvania.
3. Haggerty, 203.
4. Due to heavy cross-fire and congestion on the beach at Dog Green, Max Schneider ordered the boats to land on Dog White and Dog Red. See Ronald Drez, Voices Of D-Day (Baton Rouge, Louisiana: Louisiana State University Press, 1994), 276.
5. Clark, 58.

Chapter 6

"I Want to Fight Them":
Men at the Pointe

Task Force A numbered only about 225 brave souls. They had been recruited from all over the United States, trained together, and now they were crossing the English Channel to face death and honor as Rangers. They were men with active lives and hopes, personalities and passions. These are but a few of the husbands, fathers, sons and brothers who fought as one on those fateful days.

* * * *

Lt. James Wilmot "Ike" Eikner, Headquarters Company, was born on December 7, 1913, to Leonard and Sarah Eikner. James joined the Mississippi National Guard in 1932 and continued serving the guard until 1935. After graduating from Blackburn University with honors, in 1935, he worked for a year at Swift &.Company. He then went to work for Southwestern Bell Telephone.

Eikner entered the Army on March 14, 1942 at Fort Sam Houston, Texas. He was assigned to the 90th Infantry Division and became a sergeant in the battalion communications platoon. In August, 1942, Eikner attended Officer's Candidate School (OCS) at Fort Benning, Georgia, and graduated in November as a 2d lieutenant, Infantry. He was assigned to 80th Infantry Division at Camp Forrest and joined the 2d Rangers on April 1, 1943, as a 1st lieutenant in communications.

Prior to D-Day, Lieutenant Eikner and a few of his communications men made many modifications to their equipment in order to adapt them for amphibious warfare. Eikner also invented a hands-free telephone that was used with good success on June 6. It consisted of a microphone worn at the throat and a head-set worn under the helmet. The wearers could communicate without even speaking by simply vibrating their vocal cords. Eikner gave Rudder a demonstration of his device while they were in England; the colonel liked the concept so much he asked Ike to make up twenty of them. They handed them out to the mortar crew: one to the observer and one to the gunner. The DUKW crew also received these radio-telephones: one to the machine-gunner at the top of the ladder, one to the driver, and one to the winch operator. Eikner also worked on an under-the-helmet radio, but lack of parts caused them to give up on this item.

Lt. James Eikner survived D-Day and the war. He returned to Southwestern Bell Telephone Company in the fall of '45. He was promoted to management with several assignments in the Plant and Engineering Departments. He is now retired and lives with his wife in Texas.[1]

* * * *

Sgt. Gene Elder, F Company, was born on October 6, 1917, at Liberal, Missouri. Elder was drafted into the Army, July 16, 1941, while working in Iowa. He was inducted into service in Nevada, Missouri. Sergeant Elder then moved to Ft. Riley, Kansas, to become part of a cavalry unit. Following basic training, he was sent to Ft. Meade, Maryland, to the 4th Cavalry.

In late February of 1943 his unit traveled to the Mojave Desert and conducted desert warfare training. While there Gene Elder answered the call for volunteers to the 2d Ranger Battalion. He trained with the unit from Camp Forrest to England. At the Pointe, Sergeant Elder commanded a mortar squad. He and his men would be awarded the Bronze Star for their action on D-Day. Elder remained with the Rangers throughout the European Theater fighting in five countries: France, Belgium, Germany, Czechoslovakia and Luxembourg.

Near the end of the war in Europe, Sergeant Elder was offered a battlefield commission to go to the Pacific Theater. He declined the offer due to injuries. Gene Elder served his Country for 4 1/2 years — 11 months of that time were spent in action. After being honorably discharged, October 28, 1945, he returned to work on the family farm in Iowa. He married and raised five children.[2]

Lt. James Eikner, age 31
HQ Company, 2d Ranger Battalion, survived
Eikner Collection

Journalist, Lt. G. K. Hodenfield was a reporter for the *Stars and Stripes* and went in at Pointe-du-Hoc. Hodenfield was a student at the University of Iowa when he volunteered for the Army on December 7, 1940. Leaving behind a wife and a baby son, Hodenfield was shipped overseas and landed in Ireland on March 2, 1942. He was immediately assigned to the U.S. Army newspaper. Although he did not

Sgt. Gene Elder, age 27
Company F, 2d Ranger Battalion
Awarded the Bronze Star for action during D-Day
Elder Coll.

have Ranger training, his military mission on June 6, 1944, was to observe the 2d Rangers at Pointe-du-Hoc and report back to his newspaper. He survived the battle and the war.

After the hostilities he worked for the Associated Press and covered the Nuremberg trials, and worked for five years in Vienna, Austria. He returned to the United States in 1951 and became an education writer for the Associated Press.[3]

* * * *

Lt. George Kerchner, Company D, was sent overseas in November, 1943, as a replacement officer. In December of '43 Kerchner volunteered to try out with the 2d Ranger Battalion. He joined the battalion while they were at Bude, England. Lieutenant Kerchner successfully withstood the arduous training to become part of Company D, 2d Ranger Battalion. On June 6, 1944, when all the company officers were killed or wounded, he took command of D Company.

For his actions at Pointe-du-Hoc, George Kerchner received the Distinguished Service Cross. Kerchner survived D-Day and the war. He remained in the Army and rose to the rank of colonel. After he retired from the Military he entered a family business and settled in Maryland.[4]

* * * *

Sgt. Jack Kuhn, Company D, was born in Altoona, Pennsylvania in 1919. At a very early age Kuhn wanted to join the military. While still in grade school he became a member of a para-military group called the Boys' Brigade. In 1935, at the age of sixteen, he signed up for 30 days at the Citizens Military Training Camp, Ft. Meade,

Maryland. After attending the CMTC Kuhn, and several of his friends, lied about their ages and enlisted in the 104th Horse Cavalry in the Pennsylvania National Guard. They were supposed to be eighteen years of age in order to join. He spent four years in the guard.

After Jack graduated from High School in 1937 he traveled to Pittsburgh to enlist in the U.S. Marine Corps. Kuhn, however, failed the color-blind test and was turned away. Discouraged, he returned to Altoona. In September, 1941, he married and worked at a railroad shop in town. A year later, March, 1942, the Army called Kuhn for service. His wife was expecting their first child, and it was difficult for him to leave even though he had been anxious to be a part of the "Big Show."

To Jack's dismay, the Army sent him to attend Camp Davis' anti-aircraft OCS school in North Carolina. The artillery training required math skills which Kuhn could not master. He washed out of this school and was transferred to Fort Meade. While passing a bulletin board Jack noticed the Army's call for volunteers for the Rangers. As a boy he had seen the movie *Rogers's Rangers* and was eager to try for this elite unit. Kuhn signed up, and the first soldier he met at the barracks was 1st Sgt. Leonard Lomell. Both men would make it through D-Day and the war. Jack was awarded the Silver Star for his actions during the Battle of Pointe-du-Hoc.

Jack Kuhn returned to Altoona and worked on the police force. He then joined the Marine Corps but remained in the States during the Korean War. Jack Kuhn was discharged and returned to his law enforcement job in Altoona.[5] He was later inducted into the U.S. Army Ranger Hall of Fame at Fort Benning, Georgia.

* * * *

Cpl. Louis Lisko, radio operator, Headquarters Company, was born in Pennsylvania in a family of Czech-Slovak descent. In 1942 Lisko worked in a steel mill but was drafted in July of '42. He was sent to the 80th Infantry Division in Nashville, Tennessee. In March, 1943, Lisko heard about the call for volunteers, and with about 29 comrades, signed on for Ranger duty. Lisko was wounded at the Pointe but survived. He was awarded a Silver Star for valor during D-Day.

After the war he returned to Pennsylvania. In his spare time Louis Lisko became the 2d Ranger's historian and collected documents pertaining to the unit. Mr. Lisko passed away in 1998. His ashes were spread on the Pointe, June 6, 1999. Len Lomell oversaw the solemn ceremony.[6]

* * * *

Born in Brooklyn, New York, on January 22, 1920, 1st Sgt. Leonard George Lomell, Company D, was adopted by Scandinavian immigrants and raised in Point Pleasant, New Jersey. They had lost their first born, a son, who died at the age of six. They were now in their fifties and their other children were grown and on their own. One of their daughters knew a sales girl who had just had a baby boy and was unable to care for him. This child was destined to become the Lomell's son.

Leonard attended college on an athletic scholarship and work program and graduated in June, 1941. Upon hearing about the bombing of Pearl Harbor, Leonard desired to enlist in the Army. He hoped to enroll in a service academy and advance

Lt. George Kerchner, Co. D, 2d Ranger Battalion, survived
Awarded Distinguished Service Cross for D-Day.
Kerchner Coll.

Sgt. Jack Kuhn, age 25 Co. D, 2d Ranger Battalion, survived
Kuhn Coll.

his education. He could not, however, obtain a birth certificate because of the adoption. While still trying to get into a military academy, Lomell was drafted, and the Army shipped him to Fort Meade, Maryland. At Fort Meade he was placed in the 76th Infantry Division, the "Liberty Bell Division." He quickly rose to the rank of platoon sergeant in the Intelligence and Reconnaissance Platoon, Headquarters Company, of the 417th Infantry Regiment.

As an I & R Platoon sergeant, the regimental commander sent him to the first Ranger school set up on U.S. soil with 200 other men from the division. The division officers intended for these men to return to the 76th Infantry Division and train the other men. Less than half of the 200 soldiers graduated from the Ranger school. Lomell was one of the proud graduates. Shortly after returning from the school, in March, '43, the brigadier general of the division called Sergeant Lomell in and asked, "How would you like to be a Ranger?" Lomell replied that he would have to talk it over with his company commander. He hesitated because he had a chance to become first sergeant in Headquarters Company, and he needed the money to help support his elderly parents.

Lomell returned to the general and asked if he had a chance to become first sergeant in the Ranger unit. He did, and on April 1, 1943, as a first sergeant, Lomell and approximately one whole company from the 76th Division transferred to and became D Company, 2d Ranger Battalion.

1st Sgt. Leonard Lomell was wounded on D-Day but survived the battle. After D-Day he was promoted to battalion sergeant-major and in October, 1944, he received a battlefield commission to lieutenant. Although wounded again, he returned safely home in 1945. He was later awarded the Distinguished Service Cross for destroying the 5 big guns at Pointe-du-Hoc and received France's highest honor, the Legion of Honor medal. England also recognized Lomell and presented him with their Military Medal for Valor. He was later inducted into the U.S. Army Ranger Hall of Fame at Fort Benning, Georgia.

When Leonard came home he attended law school at Rutgers University under the G.I. Bill and practiced law in New Jersey after passing the bar exam in 1951. Eventually he established his own firm and became senior partner. His firm consists of sixteen lawyers and more than thirty other employees. It continues to operate after 42 years, and Len still serves as special council.

Len Lomell has been married to his wife, Charlotte, for 53 years. They reside in Toms River, New Jersey. Len and Charlotte have 3 daughters, 4 grandchildren and 2 great-grandchildren.[7]

* * * *

In May, 1921, William "L-Rod" Petty was born in Cohutta, Georgia. A few of Bill's relatives had fought in the Civil War — some for the North, others for the South. He was very bright and received a scholarship to the University of Georgia. Petty volunteered for military duty in 1941. Subsequently, he saw the call for recruits to the 2d Rangers, and he eagerly applied. He was a pale-faced, unimposing kid whose top teeth had been knocked out during a football game; Colonel Rudder was not impressed and turned him down, twice.

When the colonel returned once again to the 80th Division to screen for additional

Cpl. Louis Lisko
HQ Co.,
2d Ranger Battalion, survived
Lisko Ranger Box, USAMHI

1st Sgt. Leonard Lomell, age 24
Co. D, 2d Ranger Battalion, survived
Lomell Coll.

volunteers, Petty was in the front row. "I thought I discouraged you, Petty," Rudder said gruffly. The colonel then commented on Petty's missing teeth. Petty replied, "I don't want to bite them, Sir, I want to fight them." Rudder gave in, and Petty joined Company F, 2d Ranger Battalion, and fight he did!

On D-Day Petty was credited for killing at least 30 enemy soldiers with his B.A.R. He was later awarded a Silver Star for his performance at the Pointe. After this battle he was wounded but was able to return to his unit and again proved himself in combat during the fight on Hill 400 and received a second Silver Star for bravery. L-Rod arrived safely back in the States. He and fellow Ranger, Herm Stein, have remained friends.[8]

* * * *

T/4 Frank South, Headquarters Company, born in Nebraska in 1924, entered the military at the end of his first year at Bradley University in Illinois. He attended basic training at Fort Jackson as a medic in the 106th Division. While there, South learned that officers were interviewing soldiers to join the Rangers. Following his interview, Frank South moved on to Camp Forrest and became a medic in the 2d Rangers. He survived the war and became a teacher in biophysics and physiology.[9]

* * * *

T/5 Herman Stein was born on April 23, 1921, and grew up in Staten Island, New York. When Congress declared war on the Axis Powers in 1941, Stein was selected for duty in the first draft. The Army placed him in the 76th Division. At one point Herman attempted to join the paratroopers, but he was rejected due to poor eyesight.

In April of '42 he saw the call for Rangers and volunteered. He earned three stripes in Company F, 2d Ranger Battalion and became good friends with William "L-Rod" Petty. Stein considered himself a civilian soldier. If a situation did not suit him or seemed unreasonable he improvised. During one climbing exercise he and his comrades were ordered to scale two separate 10 foot sections of cliff. The ropes hung free, and it was impossible to get a foot-hold. Although they were ordered to keep their equipment on, Herm took his gear off and scrambled up the rope; another comrade followed his example. At the top the men jockeyed the ropes to a more favorable position for the rest of the men. Their captain, Otto Masny, quietly praised Stein for making the right move.

In another training session Stein and his platoon comrades did not work up to their potential; they, in fact, were goofing off. Lt. Jacob Hill angrily yelled at the platoon, "You guys want to goof off, fine! Now, all of you do the hokey-pokey." The F Company Rangers thought Hill was joking, but to their dismay he was not. While in their uniforms (signifying to the world their rugged manliness), out in an open field, Stein and his comrades performed the silly dance. They learned their lesson that day and straightened up.

When the 2d Battalion moved to Ft. Dix, New Jersey, Herm was overjoyed because he was only a few hours away from home. Just before the unit was shipped overseas he called his high school sweetheart, Lena. "Do you want to get married?"

Stein bluntly stated when she answered the phone. Lena said, "yes;" they have been married for 56 years.

On D-Day T/5 Herman Stein successfully scaled the cliffs and survived two days of intense fighting, but his good friend, Jack Richards, was killed.[10] Herm was later wounded at Hill 400 and was awarded the Distinguished Service Cross for his action during this battle. "L-Rod really got me the award. He should have received it," Herm later commented. "I don't brag about it. I was doing my job, but I'm not ashamed of it either," Stein added. In 1945 Herman returned to the States and his wife, Lena, who remains "the love of his life."[11]

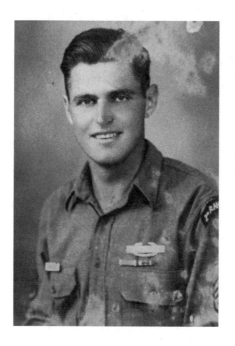

T/5 Herman Stein, age 23
Co. F, good friends with "L-Rod;" both made
it through the war.
Herm Stein Coll.

T/ Sgt. William "L-Rod" Petty, age 23
Co. F, rejected by Col. Rudder
twice but finally convinced the
colonel to allow him to join the
2d Ranger battalion. He killed
at least 30 Germans on the Pointe.
Herm Stein Coll.

* * * *

Sgt. Sigurd Sundby, Company D, was inducted into the Army in September 1942. He was sent to Camp McCauley and worked in the commissary because he had poor eye sight in his left eye. Bored with this duty, Sundby asked to be reassigned. When he went for his physical he passed the eye test because he had memorized the eye chart. Since he passed the test, he was put in the 76th Infantry Division, 304th

Infantry Regiment. It was at this time that officers came seeking volunteers for the new Ranger outfit. About 500 men from the division volunteered, but the Ranger lieutenant and sergeant put them through extreme physical trials. The next day the group had dwindled to about 250. At the end of a few weeks, only 50 men were left, and the Rangers only wanted 17. Sundby made it; he was assigned to Company D, 2d Rangers. He became a sergeant and won the Silver Star for his bravery at Hill 400, Germany, December 7, 1944. Sundby survived the war.[12]

* * * *

Lt. Elmer Vermeer, Headquarters, was born in Pella, Iowa on June 7, 1920. He grew up on a farm and worked hard. In the spring of 1942 while in the Army he was asked to attend Officers' Candidate School at Belvoir, Virginia. He was commissioned a second lieutenant and sent to the 2d Division in Louisiana and was subsequently assigned to the 2d Engineer Battalion. In the Engineers he became a platoon commander of Company B. During the Spring and Summer of '43 they worked on studying amphibious landings and building bridges under combat circumstances.

Late that summer, Lieutenant Vermeer's unit traveled to Ireland where they practiced more bridge building and gained experience with demolitions, amphibious landings and assaults. While in Ireland a recruiter from the 2d Rangers asked him if he would like to become an engineer officer for the 2d. Lieutenant Vermeer jumped at the offer, and the 2d Rangers gained another officer for Headquarters. Vermeer passed the commando training and joined the Rangers at Bude, England. He then went through the intense cliff-climbing exercises. Vermeer went in on D-Day; he survived.[13]

Notes to Chapter 6:

[1] James W. Eikner, "A Bit of Biodata," sent to the author June 17, 1999.

[2] Gene Elder oral history, the Eisenhower Center, New Orleans, Louisiana.

[3] G. K. Hodenfield, Testimony, in Sylvie Chapelie's "The American Example: Overlord," 171-172, 2d Ranger Box 1, Photo Archives, United States Military History Institute, Carlisle Barracks, Carlisle, Pennsylvania.

[4] George Kerchner, oral history, the Eisenhower Center, New Orleans, Louisiana. See also Gerald Astor, *June 6, 1944: The Voices Of D-Day* (New York, New York: St. Martin's Press, 1994), 364.

[5] Astor, 43-44, 364.

[6] Chapelie, Lou Lisko's Testimony, 171. Conversation with Len Lomell July, 1999.

[7] Leonard Lomell, oral history, the Eisenhower Center, New Orleans, Louisiana, 1-5. See also Astor, 364.

[8] Phone Interview with Herman Stein, July 18, 1999. See also, Heinz, "I took my Son to Omaha Beach . . .", 27.

[9] Astor, 45, 364.

[10] Jack was a Pittsburgh Steeler who had a promising career. He might have waited for the draft, but he chose to enlist.

[11] Phone Interviews with Herman Stein, July 18, 1999 and August 18, 1999.

[12] Drez, 30.

[13] *Ibid.*, 31-32.

Chapter 7

"May God Be With You":
Crossing the Channel

D-Day had been set for June 5, 1944. On June 1 the men were brought by
truck to Weymouth and Plymouth, England.[1] The huge, Allied armada had been
gathering on the south-east corner of Britain since late May. Approximately 175,000
soldiers would be transported across the English Channel; 5,333 ships would
participate taking needed personnel and supplies; 11,000 airplanes would bomb and
transport airborne paratroopers and paragliders into Normandy. It was an awe inspiring
sight. But the massive numbers could not hide from the prying eyes of the German
Luftwaffe.

   Just prior to boarding their troop ships, while still in a marshaling area,
German bombers hit the port near the Rangers. T/4 William Weber, HQ Company,
remembered the bombs raining down on his unit.

> . . . It was here we got our first taste of action and what we could
> expect. The planes could be heard over the harbor but no one gave
> it a thought that it was the enemy until the first flares were dropped.
> Search lights began winging about the sky in that erratic way of
> theirs and the red lines of tracers began to crisscross as the ships in
> the harbor and the shore batteries of Ack-ack opened up. It was
> then one could hear that high whine that signals the Stuka in its
> dive. Men took off in all directions for the cover of their fox holes.
> The bombs fell in a nearby area giving everyone a shaking up and
> killing a couple of MPs on duty. The attack was a long, drawn out
> affair and it was a nerve-tense outfit that finally hit the sack.[2]

Lieutenant Eikner, Weber's superior, also recalled the tense moments:

> . . . I can remember when the eggs began to fall I rushed out of our
> tar paper HQ and rushed to a trench that I had expected to use and
> lo and behold it was filled with GI's already so all I could do was to
> flatten out on the ground and keep my fingers crossed and thankfully
> everything came out all right.[3]

   After surviving the German bombs, the entire 2d Battalion came down with
food poisoning. It was bad enough having to contend with one's nerves before a
battle, now the food which they had been served was rancid. The whole battalion
was laid low, and many began to doubt if they could go ahead with their mission.
Some even suspected that their food had been tampered with. They had been served
hot dogs the night before.[4]

   For the most part the men quickly recovered from the food poisoning and
waited anxiously for their orders. Finally, on June 4, the word came to board the *Ben*

The Liberation of Pointe du Hoc

Machree, Prince Charles, and *Amsterdam.* It rained very hard that day, but it wasn't until much later in the afternoon that the Rangers were informed that the invasion was postponed. To keep busy the men played poker and told stories. Tension rose again as German Stuka dive bombers attacked the armada, but no Ranger ships were hit.[5]

* * * *

In the mother ships the men also used this time to check and recheck their equipment: ammunition, weapons, food — chocolate, D-rations — and gas masks. The men were crowded below decks, officers and enlisted men alike. Each soldier was weighted down with equipment and gear. The Rangers' gear included a steel helmet with no netting or camouflage cloth on it. Most of the Rangers had their chin straps hooked up on the back lip of their helmet. The consensus was that if a shell hit nearby, and the chin strap was under your chin, the concussion from the shell could lift the helmet from the head spraining the neck and/or killing the soldier. On the other hand, if the chin strap was not worn, the concussion would harmlessly blow the helmet from off one's head. Their theory was not valid, but this is what the men commonly thought at the time. Not using the chin strap, however, created problems for the Rangers. When they ran they had to hold their helmet on with one hand and carry their weapon in the other.

The officers wore black insignia of rank on the front of their helmets. This was to prevent the insignia from being recognized from a distance but could be easily seen up close. On the back of the Rangers' helmets was painted an orange diamond. The diamonds were about 4 or 5 inches long and about 2 1/2 inches high. The 2d Rangers had a number "2" printed in the middle of the diamond. Non-commissioned officers also had a horizontal white stripe, 3 inches long and 3/4 of an inch high painted on the back of the helmet.

A Ranger diamond patch with the word "Ranger" was sewn on their left, upper sleeve. The battle dress they wore was heavy herring-bone twill. The jackets were new and impregnated with a chemical that was supposed to counter any blister gases — mustard or lewisite. They were heavy and stiff. The chemical prevented the cloth from breathing; therefore, the men sweated in them by day and froze in them at night. To make matters worse, the men were told not to wash them. After wearing them through the salt water, sweating in them, getting them full of mud, sand and everything else, the clothing became quite putrid.

The pants issued were standard issue olive green infantry pants. Some Rangers, however, wore paratroopers trousers. These pants had large pockets on the thighs which allowed the soldier to carry more ammunition and grenades.

Most of the men left their combat packs on the supply landing craft. In their pockets and around their cartridge belt they carried just about everything they would need — D-bars, ammo, grenades and cigarettes. Officers stuffed their valuable field maps in their pockets. The enlisted men, and some officers, also took entrenching tools. Everyone was issued a gas mask which they tied to their waist and left leg. A few soldiers put extra food inside these masks. Cartridge belts were worn around the waist. One canteen of water was strapped to their belt. Every man carried a section of toggle rope around them; each soldier had a length of about six feet. The theory was, if they got stuck they could hook the ropes together.[6]

For foot gear, the officers wore paratroopers' boots. Many of the enlisted soldiers wore these as well. Others donned a high shoe with cut down leggings (gaiters) which were about six inches high.[7]

To help keep the men afloat, life jackets, "Mae West's," or CO_2 life belts were handed out to the men.

Like their clothing, new weapons were issued to the soldiers. The Rangers were issued Tommy guns, M-1 rifles, carbines, B.A.R.s (Browning Automatic Rifles), bazookas, mortars and machine guns. These guns were test-fired and zeroed in on the firing range. Ammunition clips were given to the soldiers. Bayonets and combat knives were also issued. Rangers grabbed several types of grenades: fragmentation grenades, impact hand grenades, and thermite grenades. Grenades were handed out by the boxful. The Thermite grenades burned white hot; they could melt metal, and they did not explode like other grenades. These would play a significant role at Pointe-du-Hoc. Smoke grenades were also taken in order to signal friendly aircraft of their location to avoid being targeted by Allied bombers.

* * * *

After compulsively checking and re-checking their equipment, the men went back to playing poker, gambling and otherwise entertaining themselves. One of the boys, Sgt. Antonio "Ruggie" Ruggiero, D Company, had done a little professional tap dancing prior to becoming a Ranger. Lieutenant Kerchner remembered ". . . He danced and various fellows would sing. I know we had a banjo or ukelele aboard ship. We did have some entertainment, I guess, just trying to cheer ourselves up."[8]

Over in F Company, Sgt. Gene Elder conducted a little more serious detail. He kept busy checking the rope which would be used to climb the steep cliffs. On the night of June 5, after they had received news that they would be going in on the 6th, Elder crawled into an LCA that was hanging in the mother ship. Elder explained what he was doing:

> I was in repairing on some rope that was to go up the next day, and another GI climbed in to see what I was doing. In doing this, he accidentally fell on one of the consoles controlling the electrical buttons and fired a rocket. It was about a 3-foot long rocket and bashed into about 150 feet of rope. Wham, bang, this hits several supports, but no serious damage resulted.[9]

In another part of the ship Sgt. Frank South, one of the medics, readied his gear and Capt. Walter "Doc" Block's medical supplies.

> . . . Since I was the biggest and presumably strong — as well as the youngest and perhaps the most naive — Block asked me to work with him putting together a very large pack of medical gear and supplies to be carried on a mountain packboard. On its horns I coiled about fifty feet of three-eighths-inch line in case I had to ditch it in the surf and pull it to shore. The pack contained plasma,

sulfa-based antibiotics — there was no penicillin yet —drugs, additional instruments, bandages, suture material, and whatever else I could think of. God knows how much it weighed, perhaps sixty-five or seventy pounds. It was a walking aid station, and I don't recall any other medic making or carrying such a pack. In addition, I carried my regular aid kit, side arm, knife, canteen, an Argus C-3 camera . . . and a D-ration bar.[10]

As Sergeant South packed his medical gear, Father Joe Lacy, the Ranger group chaplain, visited Rudder's three companies, all of whom were scheduled to hit the Pointe. Lacy conducted services for the Catholics and Protestants. Between playing games and checking equipment, Lieutenant Kerchner recalled being very glad Father Lacy visited their ship. He was a fat, little Irishman but a

> . . . real wonderful man. He was sort of given to us just a few weeks before D-Day . . . I know it was a surprise, I hope a pleasant surprise to him but he hadn't done the strenuous training that we had had, and I know he was worried about being able to keep up with us. But one of the things that I remember him saying to all of us on D-Day, at least the people aboard the ship that always stuck in my mind, he said, "When you land on the beach and you get in there I don't want to see anybody kneeling down and praying. If I do I'm gonna come up and boot you in the tail. You leave the praying to me and you do the fighting."[11]

While Chaplain Lacy provided spiritual comfort for Companies D, E and F, Rudder went aboard the *Prince Charles* to give Companies, A, B, and C a quick pep talk. He stood up and told his Rangers,

> . . . Boys, you are going on the beach as the first rangers in this battalion to set foot on French soil. But don't worry about being alone. When D, E, and F take care of Pointe-du-Hoc, we will come down and give you a hand with your objectives. Good luck and may God be with you.[12]

Rudder then returned to the *HMS Ben Machree*.

Lieutenant Colonel Rudder had earlier been ordered by the American general in charge of Omaha Beach, Lt. Gen. Clarence Huebner, 1st Infantry Division commander, not to go into battle with his battalion. "We're not going to risk getting you knocked out in the first round," General Huebner had stated. Rudder politely but respectfully refused, "I'm sorry to have to disobey you, sir, but if I don't take it, it may not go." And, with that, General Huebner did not force the issue.[13]

* * * *

Lieutenant Colonel Rudder continued to prepare his companies for the invasion. One of the major problems was that in order to climb the steep cliffs they could not carry a lot with them. At the same time, they had to make sure that they carried enough equipment to repulse counterattacks from the Germans.

On the night of June 5th their supplies and equipment were checked one last time. It was a very dark night; the sea slammed furiously against the rocking ships. Lieutenant Kerchner played a game of bridge and went to bed around 10:30 or 11:00 p.m. Some men awoke to the dull drone of airplanes flying overhead. Bombs could be heard dropping on the Normandy coast.[14] The British crew came around about 3:00 a.m. and awoke the Rangers. They quietly got dressed and went to the forward hold to eat breakfast: one flap jack, with no grease, and a cup of coffee was served to the Rangers. The men cracked jokes about the condemned eating their last meal.[15] Many soldiers, however, could not eat. They were too seasick.

Following breakfast, they gathered their gear and waited for the announcement to board the LCAs. They had rehearsed for this moment and now the Big Show was about to start. But it was all too real as they stood anticipating the order. Pvt. Salva Maimone, Company E, recounted the complete hopelessness he felt:

> . . . we were facing great odds. The way . . . [the junior officers] put it to you, you really don't have a chance, and with the odds you had there, it made life like you were ready to go to the electric chair, because you were on the boat, and you tried to forget about it, but it went on . . . the officers said that anyone that even gets close to the cliffs ought to get an award.[16]

The suspense and dread and hope which possess men during such moments cannot be adequately told.

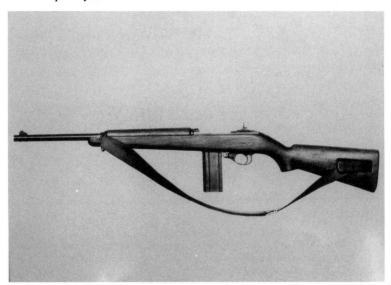

M1 Carbine, USAMHI
Operation: Semiautomatic, gas operated (750-775 r.p.m.); Caliber: .30; Feeding Mechanism and Capacity: 15 round and 30 round detachable box magazines; Weight 5 pounds.

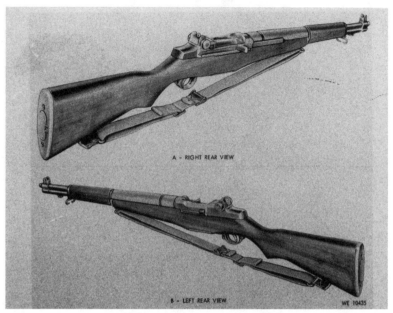

M1 "Garand" Rifle, USAMHI
Operation: Semiautomatic, gas operated; Caliber: .30; Feeding Mechanism and Capacity: Eight round internal magazine fed by an eight round clip which is ejected after the last round has been fired; Weight: 9.5 pounds.

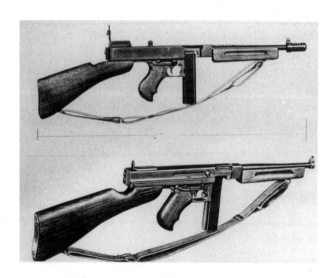

Thompson Submachine Gun, USAMHI
Operation: Selevtive fire, full automatic and semiautomatic. Caliber .45. Feeding mechanism and capacity: M1928A1, 50 round detachable drum, 20 and 30 round detachable box magazines. M1 and M1A1, 20 and 30 round detachable box magazines. Weight: M1928A1, 11 pounds. M1 and M1A1, 10 pounds 7 ounces. Rate of fire: automatic, M1928A1, 600-725 rpm. M1 and M1A1, 700-800 rpm.

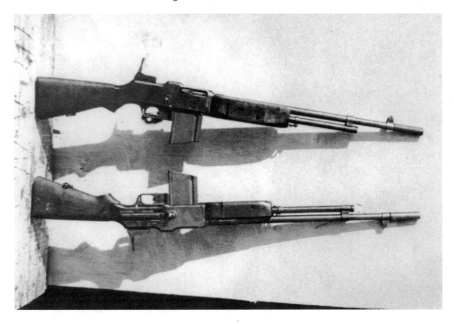

Browning Automatic Rifle (B.A.R.), USAMHI
Operation: M1918 and M1918A1, Selective fire, gas operated, semiautomatic and fully automatic, M1918A2, semiautomatic and fully automatic; Caliber: .30; Feeding Mechanism and Capacity: 20 round detachable box magazine; Weight: M1918, 16 pounds, M1918A1, 18.5 pounds, M1918A2, 19.4 pounds; Rate of fire: M1918 and M1918A1, semiautomatic and fully automatic at approximately 550 rounds per minute (r.p.m.). M1918A2, fully automatic, 300-450 r.p.m. (slow rate), 500-650 r.p.m. (fast rate). An assistant usually accompanied a B.A.R. man and carried additional ammunition.

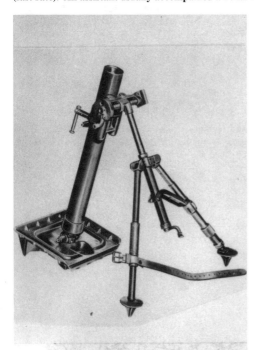

60mm M2 Mortar, USAMHI
Weight: 42 lbs.
Muzzle velocity (HE): 535 fps. Maximum Range (HE): 1,985 yds.
Rate of fire: 18 rpm normal, 30 - 35 maximum.
A three man crew operated this weapon..

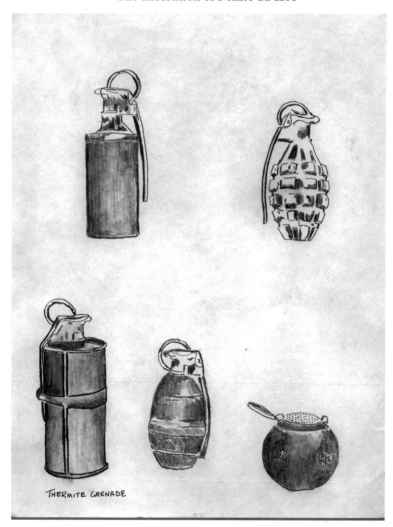

THERMITE GRENADE

Clockwise, from top left: Mk1 Offensive Hand Grenade, Mk2 Fragmentation Grenade, TH14 Incendiary (Thermite) Grenade, Mk1 Illuminating Grenade, T13 Impact Grenade. USAMHI

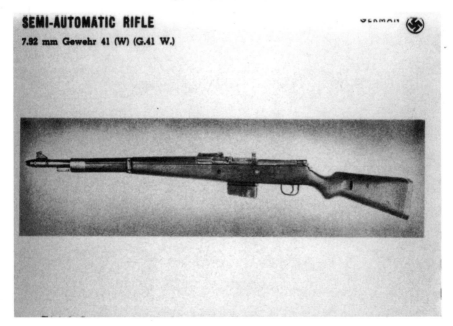

SEMI-AUTOMATIC RIFLE

7.92 mm Gewehr 41 (W) (G.41 W.)

Gewehr 41 rifle, Enemy Ordnance Material
Operation: semiautomatic, gas-operated, air-cooled. Caliber: 7.92mm, fixed vertical box, 10 rounds staggered. Weight: 10.5 lbs.

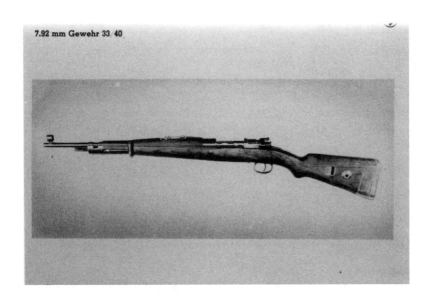

7.92 mm Gewehr 33/40

Gewehr 33/40 carbine, Enemy Ordnance Material
Manually operated, bolt action, air-cooled. Caliber: 7.92mm; five round, clip-fed, hand-loaded magazine. Weight: 7 lbs, 11 ounces.

9 mm M. P. 38 and M. P. 40 (Schmeisser)

This submachine gun was originally designed for use by **SPECIFICATIONS**

Submachine Gun (Schmeisser) M.P. 38 and M.P. 40, *Enemy Ordnance Material*
Operation: air-cooled, blowback operated; Caliber: 9mm (.347 in.); Feeding mechanism and capacity: 32 round box magazine; Weight: with magazine, 10 pounds 7 ounces; Range: 200 yards; Rate of fire: practical, 80 to 90 r.p.m., cyclic, 518 r.p.m. Americans nick-named this the "burp" gun.

SUBMACHINE GUN

GERMAN

7.92 mm M. P. 43, M. P. 43 1, M. P. 44 (Sturmgewehr 44)

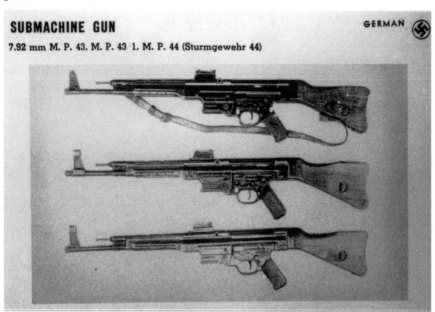

Submachine Gun (Sturmgewehr 44) Top: M.P. 43; Center: M.P. 43/1; Bottom: M.P. 44. *Enemy Ordnance Material* Operation: Automatic, gas operated, air-cooled; Caliber: 7.92 (.312 in); feeding mechanism and capacity: curved 30 round magazine; Weight: 10 pounds 7 ounces; Rate of fire: automatic, 100-200 r.p.m., semiautomatic, 45 to 50 r.p.m.

NEW TYPE STICK HAND GRENADE
Stielhandgranate 43

GERMAN

The new type German Stick Grenade, consisting of a head filled with TNT, a smooth fragmentation sleeve, fitted over the head, and a detachable wooden handle, is a modification of the standard Stielhandgranate 24 described on page 321.

The later model, however, does not have a friction igniter operated by a cord running through the handle. Instead, the detonator and 4½-second delay igniter similar to that used with the egg grenade, are screwed into the top of the explosive head. The grenade may be thrown with or without the handle. Arming and priming are the same as for the egg grenade.

Stick hand grenade model 24. *Enemy Ordnance Manual*

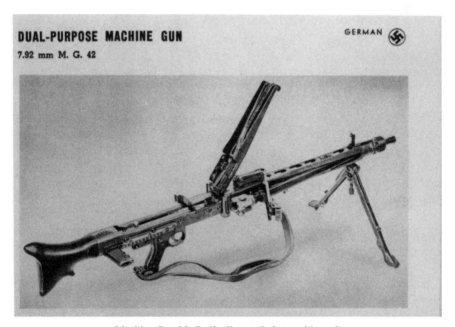

DUAL-PURPOSE MACHINE GUN
7.92 mm M. G. 42

GERMAN

Machine Gun M. G. 42. *Enemy Ordnance Manual.*

Operation: Gas operated, air-cooled, recoil-operated; Caliber: 7.92 mm (.312 in.); Feeding Mechanism and Capacity: metallic non-disintegrating link belt, 50 round lengths and multiples thereof and 50 round belt drums; Weight: with bipod, 26 pounds, with heavy machine gun tripod mounting, 65 1/2 pounds; Maximum range: 2,200 yards; effective range: 600 yards; Rate of fire: cyclic, 1,335 r.p.m. This gun fired so quickly that it sounded like one, long continuous burst; however, it quickly overheated. An extra barrel was carried by the assistant machine-gunner. The crew used asbestos pad to handle the first barrel and quickly exchange it for a new one. This weapon was so feared by opposing troops that the U.S. Army made a training film for new recruits to combat its psychological impact.

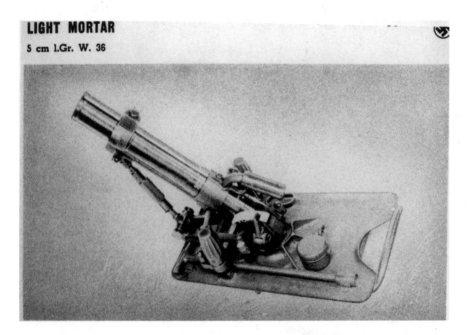

LIGHT MORTAR

5 cm l.Gr. W. 36

Light Mortar 1.Gr. W.36. *Enemy Ordnance Material*
Mount cradle and base plate, no bipod. Easily broken down into two loads for transport. Caliber:
50 mm; Ammunition: H.E. equipped with fin assembly, point-detonating fuze, and booster, Wt.
2.00 pounds; Firing Mechanism: trigger operated; Method of loading: muzzle; Weight: 31 pounds;
Range: maximum, 45 degree elevation, 550 yards; minimum, 85 degree elevation, 50 yards.

Notes to Chapter 7

[1] Elder, 2.
[2] Clark, 56.
[3] Eikner, 6.
[4] *Ibid.*
[5] *Ibid.*
[6] Kerchner, 9.
[7] For clothing see Capt. John C. Raaen, Jr., 5th Rangers, Oral History, Eisenhower Center,
5-6.
[8] Kerchner, 8.
[9] Elder, 2-3.
[10] Astor, 179.
[11] Kerchner, 7-8. Father Lacy did not land at the Pointe but went in on Dog White-Dog Green sector. During the battle he walked back and forth under fire and dragged the wounded men away from the water's edge. He also sat near many of the dying and prayed with them. He received the Distinguished Service Cross for his action on D-Day. See Kerchner, 8 and Ambrose, 429.
[12] Ambrose, 398.
[13] W. C. Heinz, "I Took My Son To Omaha Beach: The Story of An American Hero's Return to Normandy," *Collier Magazine*, June 11, 1954, 25.
[14] Unknown to the men of the 29th Infantry Division who were scheduled to land on Omaha Beach, very few of the Allies' bombs dropped on the enemy position where two German divisions lay in wait.
[15] Chapelie's, *The American Example: Overlord*, G. K. Hodenfield's Testimony, 158.
[16] Drez, 264.
[17] Caption text in Bruce N. Canfield's *U. S. Infantry Weapons of World War II* (Lincoln, Rhode Island: Andrew Mowbray Publishers, 1994), 282-289.
[18] Information on German weapons, U.S. Government, *Enemy Ordnance Manual* (Office Chief of Ordnance, 1945), 124-321.

Chapter 8

"Rangers! Man Your Craft!":
Running the Gauntlet

Five minutes after 4:00 a.m. a British officer called out on the public address system: "Rangers! Man your craft!" The loud speaker made the voice sound harsh and metallic, but the Rangers seemed to keep up their spirits. Each man braced himself for a supreme effort fearful in all its possibilities.

"All aboard for Hoboken ferry! Leaving in five minutes!" a nervous Ranger yelled out to his comrades; an uproar of laughter resounded on the mother ship.[1] An officer shot back, "Cut the chatter and get the lead out! You want to be left behind?"[2]

The three companies, and part of Headquarter's Company, boarded their 11 landing craft. Each boat carried about twenty-two men and supplies. One company filled about three boats, and two LCAs were completely full of equipment and supplies. As the men waited they saw the whole sky light up with flares and bursting shells. Wave after wave of planes could be heard, if not seen. Excitement and expectancy were now at their highest pitch. The British LCAs on the troop ships, with all men and equipment on board, were lowered into the sea by ropes and pulleys.

* * * *

Awaiting H-Hour, the British LCAs circled. The English Channel rocked and churned as the small vessels bobbed up and down like tin cans in a tempest. The mother ships had anchored about 12 miles out, and the sea was still very rough. American bombers continued to hit the Pointe up to 6:25 a.m.[3] To time the landing with H-Hour (6:30 a.m.) the order was given to form up side by side and head for shore; it was 4:30 a.m.

* * * *

LCA 914: Supply craft

From the start supply craft LCA 914 began taking on water. The vessel ran at half-speed and fell behind the other boats. Finally, water swamped its bow, and the crew was forced to abandon her. The men jumped into the sea wearing all their equipment. Pfc. Francis J. Connelly's life belt did not seem to hold him afloat. A comrade, Pfc. John J. Riley, grabbed for his buddy, but Connelly went under and did not come back up. Riley looked around and saw three other Rangers still treading water. The four agreed to try and stay together. Seeing the British coxswain and another English sailor in trouble, Pfc. Riley swam to their aid. The huge waves and current soon separated the group. Losing sight of his friends, Riley swam toward the battleship *Texas*. Four hours later, *Texas* crewmen rescued an exhausted and cold Pfc. John Riley. The other Rangers on LCA 914 went to unknown graves.[4]

Lieutenant Hodenfield, the correspondent for *Stars and Stripes*, in LCA 883, a Company F boat team, had started out joking and laughing, but when they began hearing screams from LCA 914 the kidding stopped. Hodenfield remembered the sergeant in front of the craft shouting:

'We're off, boys . . . and this time it's really the forty-nine-cent tour!'
By the time we found fairly comfortable positions in the heavily loaded
boats, the first glow of dawn was showing. The laughing and joking
was still going on, but it stopped abruptly when we saw another craft
overturn in the heavy waves just behind us. There was nothing we
could do to help those poor guys; just say a little prayer that they
would be picked up before they froze to death. We all wanted to help,
but the success of our mission was too vital, and the Rangers knew
they were expendable.[5]

* * * *

LCA 860: Capt. Harold Slater, Company D

Landing Craft 860 also experienced trouble early on. The four-foot choppy
waves swamped the vessel; D Company's commander, Capt. Harold "Duke" Slater, with
25 of his soldiers, went down. Slater and most of his men were more fortunate than
some for they were immediately picked up; however, four of the men were lost.[6] The
captain called for dry clothes and replacement weapons and ammunition; he and his
men wanted to go to the Pointe. "We gotta get back!" Captain Slater yelled. The ship's
doctor examined the men and ordered them to return to England to be hospitalized.
They were numb and suffering from hypothermia; the freezing Channel waters could be
as deadly as the German shells and bullets.[7]

* * * *

LCA 668: 1st Sgt. Len Lomell, 2d Platoon, Company D

Prior to the invasion, and while eagerly waiting on the troop ship, the three D
Company boat teams had made a $100 wager concerning which team would first reach
and take out their assigned gun positions. When 1st Sergeant Lomell's boat team saw
Slater's vessel sinking they all cheered with a careless disregard for the dangers which the
dark English Channel could generate. But even their vessel was not immune to the
waves, and every man on Lomell's boat team soon began bailing out water.[8]

* * * *

LCA 888: Lt. Col. James Rudder, HQ personnel and Company E

It seemed the devilish English Channel did not spare any of the boats in the
small flotilla. Soon after plunging into the frigid Channel, water began seeping into
Lieutenant Colonel Rudder's LCA 888. Nevertheless, it maintained its position at the
front of the column — speeding ever closer to the deadly shore line.

With two craft already gone, and the remaining nine taking on water, it seemed
they would never reach the coast. To compound the situation, Rudder, squinting and
wiping ocean spray from his face, looked ahead. Something was wrong. When he got
his first clear glance at the beach he realized they were off course about three miles. The
current had pulled them too far to the left; they were heading right for Pointe-et-Raz-de-
la-Percee — Company C's, 2d Rangers' sector. Rudder convinced the boatswain to turn

the boat to the right and head for Pointe-du-Hoc.

* * * *

LCA 668: Sgt. Leonard Lomell, Company D

1st Sergeant Lomell also realized that they were heading in the wrong direction. He called back to Sgt. Jack Kuhn, "Hey, Jack, look at this! What the hell's going on? That's not the Pointe. That's C Company's target . . . ."

Kuhn replied, "You're right, Len . . . I wonder what's up . . . ."[9]

Nothing was up except the plans were falling apart. Having wasted valuable time, the 9 boats at last sped toward Pointe-du-Hoc. The flotilla was now turned parallel to the cliffs providing the Germans with excellent targets. Bullets and artillery shells exploded in the midst of the vessels, ripping through the thin-skinned boats, throwing splinters and fragments of iron among the men.

* * * *

LCA 722: HQ and Company E

Over in LCA 722 the men paid close attention to the water pouring into their vessel. Lt. James W. Eikner, HQ Company, and the other men ripped up the floor boards in order to bail out the water with their helmets.[10] The situation got worse when men began throwing up. Lieutenant Eikner described the scene:

> . . . a little later on, while being shot at — you can imagine the situation there — with . . . bailing water with your helmet, dodging bullets and vomiting all at the same time, not much fun I can assure you.[11]

Moving closer to shore the Germans opened on the Rangers with an intense barrage of artillery and small arms fire. Lieutenant Eikner continued with his description:

> . . . Just about day break all hell broke out . . . we were within small arms range, and I can remember when the first small arms hit our boat and it made a noise and somebody said, 'what is that?' and we looked up and there was a little round hole through one of the rope boxes. And I said, 'my god these guys are playing for keeps,' and so we all got down, and we had been standing up except for those who were bailing water — so we all ducked down. The Germans were taking us under fire like shooting ducks in a tub, and it got worse as we got closer to the Pointe. I can recall at one time we were fired on by 20mm guns firing incendiary, and you look up and see this big ball of fire coming. Fortunately none of — or rather, my craft was not hit.[12]

One of the amphibious trucks — a DUKW — was hit and several of the men on the truck were killed. Screams of pain and terror pierced the air.

Cpl. Lou Lisko was also in LCA 722. When within 70 yards of the cliff, Pfc. John J. Sillmon was hit by a bullet in the upper left chest. Blood spewed everywhere; Sillmon began groaning and moaning. Lisko recalled the horrifying scene:

> . . . Bullets from machine guns and rifles were flying in the air from the top of the Hoc and nobody dared to help him . . . Another ranger sitting by my side got sick. Though we all had paper bags under our field jackets near the throat to vomit [into], this man did not have time to reach it, and he vomited all over my left leg, my carbine and radio equipment. I don't know why he vomited so much because all we ate was one pancake, without grease, and a cup of coffee three hours earlier. But that made me sick too, and I vomited in my paper bag and threw it overboard.[13]

* * * *

LCA 858: Lt. Kerchner, Company D

In order to provide cover fire for the Ranger flotilla the battleship *Texas* and two destroyers, USS *Satterlee* and HMS *Talybont*, pummeled the Pointe. Special rockets mounted on crafts were also unleashed. Lieutenant Kerchner, D Company, LCA 858, recalled the enormous power of the battleship's guns and rockets:

> . . . [a] terrifying sound it was when they started firing their 14 inch guns. Of course they were passing far over our heads, but we were close enough to hear and feel some of the muzzle blasts. I recall as we got perhaps half way in, one of the rocket-firing craft that was off of Omaha beach fired their . . . rockets. This was also a terrifying thing; I think there was a thousand or more rockets on these landing craft, and they fired in salvos of maybe 10 or 15 at a time. It was just one continuous sheet of fire going up from this rocket-firing craft . . . I remember wondering how could anybody really live on the beaches with all of this fire that was [presumably] landing there, ...[14]

The earth and elements trembled with the deadly shock of combat. A few of the rockets landed short among Rudder's LCAs; someone had the wrong range, and now the men were in danger from both sides.

* * * *

LCA 884: Lt. Jacob J. Hill, Company F

Ducking and taking cover from this mind-numbing fusillade was not the style of all members of the landing crafts. Lt. Jacob J. Hill's Company F team, on LCA 884, was enduring a terrible fire from German infantrymen; however, Hill's men stood up and replied with their small arms and B.A.R.s. The Germans ran for shelter.[15]

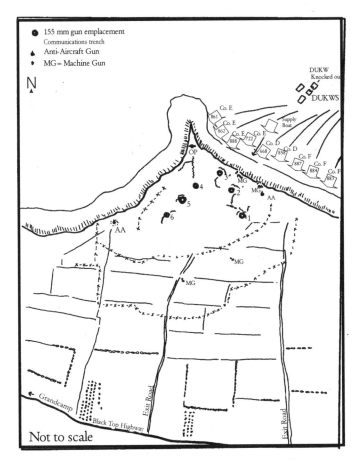

Map 4: Where the nine LCAs landed on June 6, 1944.

* * * *

LCA 883: Capt. Otto "Big Stoop" Masny, Company F

F Company's other boat team, with their commander on it, Capt. Otto Masny in LCA 883, trailed behind the little armada. Journalist Lt. G. K. Hodenfield noted,

> . . . As we watched the coast of France draw nearer and nearer, it didn't seem possible that this was really the invasion, the second front for which so many men had trained for so long. It looked peaceful, too quiet. But suddenly we heard a sharp rat-ta-tat, and we saw machine gun bullets fall into the water ahead of us.[16]

A Ranger on Hodenfield's craft yelled out, "Hey boss! Those jerks are trying to hit us!" It was the understatement of the day.

* * * *

Company F:

On T/Sgt. Tom Ryan's boat the scene was surreal. "The fellows sang 'Happy Birthday' to me in the boat coming over to Pointe-du-Hoc," Tom later wrote. Sergeant Ryan was spending his 22d Birthday on an LCA moving into a hail of bullets and artillery fire. He lived to see another birthday and many more.[17]

* * * *

Off course, the LCAs approached the Pointe from the east. Two of the LCAs from Company D were scheduled to land on the west side of the cliffs, but they were signaled to proceed ahead. Now all nine LCAs and two DUKWs jammed onto the east shore (see map 4).

Notes on Chapter 8

[1] Chapelie, Hodenfield's testimony, 158.

[2] Lane, 1.

[3] Chapelie, Lisko's testimony, 135.

[4] Lane, 7.

[5] Chapelie, Hodenfield's testimony, 159.

[6] Lomell's Oral History, 4.

[7] Lane, 78.

[8] Interview with Len Lomell, August 21, 1999. The survivors of Lomell's boat team learned later that four men had drowned from Captain Slater's boat team.

[9] *Ibid.*, 79.

[10] Phone conversation with James W. Eikner, July 25, 1999. Eikner stated that at the last moment Rudder decided not have so many HQ personnel in LCA 888. James recalled that he probably rode in LCA 722.

[11] Eikner, 8.

[12] *Ibid.*, 9.

[13] Chapelie, Lisko's testimony, 136.

[14]. Kerchner, 10.

[15] Lane, 89.

[16] Chapelie, Hodenfield's testimony, 160.

[17] Tom Ryan, "Celebration in France Makes Another Memorable Birthday." <http://web.lexisnexis.com/universe/doc...3&_md5=9cee4db1e8178315aa63253fbe17eald>. June 6, 1994 *Chicago Sun-Times, Inc.*

Chapter 9

"All Right, Everybody Out":
Climbing the cliffs

LCA 888: HQ and Company E

The nine LCAs hit the shore around 7:10 a.m., approximately a half-an-hour late. Their front covered 500 yards, and, although crowded, they were evenly spaced. Rudder's craft landed first. His radio operator, T/5 Francis "Killer" J. Kolodziejczak, HQ Company, four other men from HQ Company and 16 men from E Company followed Rudder.

When the vessel reached an appropriate distance the rockets with grapple hooks and attached rope ladders were fired. They unleashed two at a time. Some of the ropes failed to make it because they were too wet and heavy; others simply fell out on the clay. The Germans rushed to cut those within reach. Rangers, however, brought additional portable rockets and fired them from the shore. The enemy now came to the bluff and commenced pouring down death and destruction on the men below.

Rangers took aim at the defenders. Sgt. Domenick B. Boggetto blasted his B.A.R. up toward the Germans; he hit one, and the man plunged over the edge. It was one of the Rangers' first kills.[1] There was no sign of flinching even at the most appalling moments: some men provided cover fire, others unloaded equipment, and a few of the Rangers on LCA 888 began to climb the cliff.

When they reached the ropes they found that the wet clay fronting them had crumbled due to the intense bombing. A mound had formed about 40 feet up the cliff; several Rangers scrambled up the dirt pile. They carried a 16 foot section of extension ladder with a toggle rope attached to the top. One of the Rangers climbed the ladder and used his bayonet to cut a foothold into the cliff. A second soldier came from behind and helped his comrade with the next section. T/5 George J. Putzek made it safely to the top and cradled the top rung of the ladder in his arms. The Germans sighted him and seriously wounded him with small arms fire, but Putzek hung on as fellow Rangers continued to climb.[2]

Rudder's boat team scrambled up to the Pointe in less than 15 minutes. When one trooper, nicknamed the "Preacher" because he was a dead shot, reached the top he immediately pulled down his pants to defecate with urgency.[3]

* * * *

LCA 861: Lt. Theodore E. Lapres, Jr., Company E

Behind LCA 888 came landing craft 861, commanded by Lt. Theordore E. Lapres, Jr., of Company E. As they approached the shore they found themselves on the far right about 25 yards from the cliff bottom. Germans zeroed in on the boat and sprayed rifle and machine gun fire down on them; others threw grenades. S/Sgt. Curtis A. Simmons and T/5 E.G. "Bud" Colvard, Jr. returned fire and drove the enemy off. Once Lapres felt the bottom of the boat scrape the beach he directed the rockets' release. The rear pair took off first; the front pairs followed. None of the ropes made it to the cliff; they were thoroughly soaked and much too heavy.

The Liberation of Pointe du Hoc

Shortly after the ropes fell short of their target, LCA 861's ramp came down; the men rushed off the boat zig-zagging their way through the bomb craters. Carrying hand rockets, the Company E Rangers reached the shore and fired the ropes; both hooks caught. Pfc. Harry W. Roberts climbed the steep cliff only to come sliding back down when the rope was either cut or came loose. Slashed by the sharp rock, Roberts began struggling up the second rope; he made it this time, but he was alone at the top of the cliff. The rope Roberts had just climbed fell free.

Lieutenant Lapres needed to get his boat team up there fast. He quickly moved to the western side of the Pointe to reconnoiter the area and found the cliff intact. The Naval and Air bombardment had not chipped away at this side. Lapres returned and led 4 or 5 men up a 20 foot mound of clay which had been knocked off the eastern side. Once at the top they threw Pfc. Roberts a rope. The private tied it tightly and then laid across it. Lapres' group successfully reached the top and immediately headed toward their objective — the observation point. They did not wait for the second group from LCA 861.

Seconds later a huge explosion occurred near the rope where Lapres' squad had just been. Dirt and debris covered the second group from Lapres' team who had been patiently waiting their turn, but the line remained firm. Five men scurried up the rope. At the top the lieutenant was already gone, so they, too, headed toward the German observation point.[4]

* * * *

LCA 862: Lt. Joseph E. Leagans, Company E

About 100 yards left of Lapres' boat team, LCA 862 carried 15 Rangers from Company E and Naval Shore Fire Control personnel. 1st Lt. Joseph E. Leagans led this squad and had directed that the ropes be fired when the vessel touched down. All six ropes were released, but only one plain rope and two toggle ropes reached the top, and then one of the toggle ropes came loose and fell back down.

With only two ropes to climb, Leagans' crew began scaling the cliff. German machine gun fire covered the area well; one Ranger fell dead and another was wounded. Two more of Leagans' men were then injured from grenades. Lieutenant Leagans, T/5 Victor J. Aguzzi and S/Sgt. Joseph J. Cleaves safely reached the top of the cliff; they took cover in a shell hole and awaited the arrival of two more Rangers. The small squad advanced to the relative safety of a German trench on their way to the big guns.[5]

* * * *

LCA 722: HQ personnel and Company E

To the left of Leagans' group, Rudder's LCA 888 had already come ashore, and about 20 yards left of LCA 888, landing craft 722 beached. This vessel carried 15 more E Company boys along with 5 Headquarters soldiers, a *Stars and Stripes* photographer, and Lt. Col. Thomas H. Trevor, a huge British commando, six-foot four inches, who had helped train the Rangers in England.

One ladder rope and one straight rope held firm in the cliff. The ramp came down, and the Rangers rushed off the boat, Lieutenant Eikner leading the way. Cpl.

Lou Lisko noted the men in front of him disembarking:

> . . . I watched up ahead and I saw some of them jumping neck-deep
> and unable to walk. When my turn came, I saw the two rangers
> ahead of me jump and disappear, so I decided to jump to the left. I
> fell chest-deep with all my equipment (radio, ammunition, carbine),
> at the same time bullets were hitting the sea water around us. I
> struggled ahead into the water towards the base of the cliffs; it was
> not far away but so difficult to reach.[6]

With shots slapping at the water all around them, T/4 Stephen A. Liscinsky reached the shore just ahead of Lisko. The two met at the base of the cliff. Liscinsky took a piece of gum from his pocket, ripped it in two and gave half to Lisko. The two men then began connecting their radios sections. T/4 Charles S. Parker, carrying the third section of the radio, soon joined the two Rangers.[7]

While Liscinsky, Lisko and Parker assembled the radio, Lieutenant Eikner helped unload the boat. He carried off a clover leaf of 60mm mortar shells; they were fairly heavy:

> . . . I ran down the ramp and in the water about up to my knees and
> headed on across what I thought was the beach and stepped into a
> shell hole that was covered with water
> . . . I went down over my head, and of course we were under fire.
> There was one machine gun especially on our left flank . . . Some
> of our people were getting hit, and I remember one young man that
> was hit three times on the landing craft and twice more on the beach
> — believe it or not that young man survived.[8]

Eikner followed three men up to the Pointe as German soldiers leaned over the edge to shoot while others threw grenades.

About two-thirds of the way up a tremendous explosion occurred. Lieutenant Eikner was convinced it was a Naval shell which had fallen short. Tons of rock and debris dropped on the lieutenant and Lieutenant Colonel Rudder. The two officers were forced back down, but Eikner caught on a ledge. He was in pain due to blood blisters on his legs. The enemy continued to blaze away at the vulnerable officers. Eikner pulled his Tommy gun out of the rubble, pointed it, 'click;' nothing happened. The weapon jammed! Lieutenant Eikner recalled his frustration:

> . . . So there I was in the grandest invasion in history with no weapon.
> I looked around and spied a youngster with a radio on his back
> down in a cave beneath Pointe Du Hoc at water level. I scrambled
> down the cliff and went to him . . . .[9]

The lieutenant made his way through the struggling, screaming, fighting and dying Rangers and the German barrage to the radio operator who was near two or three wounded men.

"Have you sent any messages," Eikner asked the young radioman.

The soldier replied, "No, sir."

Lieutenant Eikner took the radio and relayed the code message, *Tilt*; it was 7:30 a.m. "Tilt" told Task Force B to land at Omaha Beach.[10] After sending the message, Eikner turned his attention to German prisoners descending the cliff.

* * * *

LCA 888 & 722: HQ personnel and Company E

Back near the mass of Rangers on the beach, Lieutenant Colonel Trevor had exited LCA 722 and began encouraging the men. Lt. Elmer Vermeer, the engineer from Iowa who had landed with Rudder's boat team, yelled out to Trevor, "How in the world can you do that when you are being fired at?"

Lieutenant Colonel Trevor quickly replied, "I take two short steps and three long ones, and they always miss me." Just then a bullet drilled right through his helmet and knocked him on his knees. Lieutenant Colonel Rudder ran to the big commando whose blood gushed over his face. Half mad with pain and anger, Trevor stood up and shouted at the German, "You dirty son of a bitch!"[11]

* * * *

LCA 722: HQ personnel and Company E

As Trevor cursed the enemy, and Lisko and his comrades continued piecing together their radio, other Rangers from LCA 722 climbed the two ropes. Only two had reached the top because they had been fired too early. One rope lay in a slight crevice and offered the men some protection; the rope ladder fell over an overhang and was exposed to flanking fire. T/5 Edward P. Smith easily ascended the cliff with the straight rope. He reached the top about four minutes after landing. Sgt. Hayward A. Robey, armed with a B.A.R., followed Smith and joined him at the edge. Hiding in a small niche, Robey opened up on the Germans; three soldiers were hit and the rest retreated. Pfc. Frank H. Peterson, who had been slightly wounded on the beach, came up and met his comrades.

Company E's mortar section set up on the beach. The cross-fire was too heavy, and the men brought their mortar closer to the cliff; however, this angle rendered the weapon useless. The Rangers saw Sgt. Regis McCloskey's supply craft coming in and assisted the crew to unload.

* * * *

Supply craft, Sgt. Regis F. McCloskey, Company F

Sergeant McCloskey and Cpl. Charles W. Korb carried boxes of ammunition off the craft. The waves were high, and the boatswain tried to steady the boat. McCloskey made several successful trips, but during one of them he fell into an underwater crater. The ammo box was lost. McCloskey wouldn't quit; he swam back to the boat for more and headed back to shore. "I'm hit," Korb yelled over the noise of battle. McCloskey dropped his load, picked up his comrade and carried him to a Company E boat carefully placing him inside.

On returning to his supply boat, the boatswain told Sergeant McCloskey that the German machine gun fire was too hot to stay in their location. They decided to pull back and try the west side of the Pointe, but firing on the west shore was heavy as well. The boatswain indicated to the sergeant that he was pulling out. McCloskey angrily argued that the boat was not yet unloaded, but the boatswain won out. Fortunately for Korb, the sailor did return to the east side to pick him up.

As Sergeant McCloskey hauled Korb back to the supply craft, the corporal was hit again in the arm. The two, however, stumbled into the boat and headed toward the battleship *Texas.* Korb received medical attention and survived.[12]

* * * *

LCA 668: 1st Sgt. Leonard Lomell, Company D

Sailors on LCA 668 saw the chaos unfolding on the east side of the Pointe. LCA 668 and LCA 858 carried Rangers from D Company. Company D's boats were to land on the west side of the cliff, but due to the confusion, and being behind schedule, they unloaded between Companies E and F.

LCA 668, commanded by 1st Sgt. Leonard Lomell, came in to the left of LCA 722. Lomell's boat grounded short of the beach due to boulders and dirt which had been knocked off into the water. Their rockets were fired; three of the six ropes carried over the cliff. 1st Sergeant Lomell recounted coming in and their initial minutes on the beach:

> . . . I landed right between them [Companies E and F] . . . I wasn't supposed to land there . . . because of running behind schedule and a lot of other things, we said "To hell with it, let's jam right in between E and F Company."

> . . . The ramp goes down; I'm the first guy shot, machine-gunned through the right side. And then I step off into water over my head . . . I came out of that water, and I have my arms full of gear and stuff. The guys pulled me out, my platoon, and I just rushed to the base of the cliff and grabbed any rope or thing that we could get our hands on to get up that cliff.[13]

Whether the bullet was from a machine gun or rifle, Lomell could not tell. He examined the injury and saw that it had grazed his side. Lomell then grabbed a rope. Two rope ladders had just barely reached the top, and the other was a toggle rope. 1st Sergeant Lomell directed Sgt. Bill Vaughan, with his B.A.R., to climb the toggle rope. Vaughan easily shinnied up the cliff. The other ropes, however, were not easy to climb. Pvt. Sigurd Sundby, recalled

> . . . the rope was wet and kind of muddy. My hands just couldn't hold; they were like grease, and I came sliding back down. I wrapped my foot around the rope and slowed myself up as much as I could, but still I burned my hands. If the rope hadn't been so wet, I wouldn't have been able to hang on for the burning.

I landed right beside Sweany [Melvin W.], and he says, 'What's the matter, Sundby, chicken? Let me — I'll show you how to climb.' So he went up first and I was right up after him. And when I got to the top, Sweany says, 'Hey, Sundby, don't forget to zigzag.'[14]

Lomell also noted that the ropes were difficult to climb, so he ordered extension ladders set up. The Rangers placed them on a high mound which had been created by the bombardment. While a group of soldiers climbed these, others made it up the toggle rope, or any other ropes they could find. The sergeant's entire boat team, 22 in all, topped the cliff around 7:20 a.m. 1st Sergeant Lomell's 2d Platoon took off in formation moving as fast as they could toward their objectives — gun positions Nos. 4, 5 and 6.[15]

* * * *

LCA 858: Lt. George Kerchner, Company D

Directly beside Lomell's vessel, Lt. George Kerchner brought in the last team for D Company on LCA 858; as mentioned previously, the other Company D boat had sunk with their captain on board — most of the men survived. When within 25-50 yards of the shore, Kerchner ordered the rockets fired.

> . . . All of our rockets fired. They were fired in sequence two at a time. I think out of the six ropes we fired up there, at least five of our ropes cleared the cliff. This was a good percentage because some of the landing crafts had a great deal of trouble. Perhaps they fired them too soon, or perhaps the seas that were shipping over the landing craft wet the ropes too such an extent that they were so heavy that they couldn't clear the cliff . . . Immediately after firing the rockets, the ramp was lowered, and we approached the beach. The idea, and the hope and desire of all of us, was that we were going to run right up on the beach, and we were going to make a dry landing. This, again, was not because we were afraid of getting wet, but because it would have kept that much . . . more weight off of our bodies in climbing this cliff . . . They dropped the ramp and the British officer in charge said, "All right, everybody out."[16]

Kerchner looked over the head of the ramp and saw at least 15 to 20 feet of water in front of them. The sea was muddy, dirty and murky, mixed with blood and the clay from the cliff — a scene of carnage and destruction. Hundreds of shell craters pock-marked the beach and left huge, dangerously deep puddles of water. The young lieutenant looked back and hollered to his men, "O.K., let's go." Kerchner was the first man off his boat and stepped directly into 8' of water in a large bomb crater. The lieutenant described the scene at this time:

> . . . I thought, "Oh, hell, here we go." My first impulse was anger because they had made us run off of this boat . . . told us . . . it was

. . . shallow water there and here I was in water over my head. I came to the surface and started doggy paddling to try and keep my head above the water and swim in to shore. Well, the men immediately behind me as soon as they saw me run off into water over my head they realized what it was, and they filed around both sides of the shell crater. And although they got their feet wet, I don't think any of them went in the water as deep as I did . . . I remember being angry because I was soaked . . . wringing wet. I turned around and I wanted to find somebody to help me cuss out the British Navy for dumping me in this eight feet of water, . . . everybody was busily engrossed in their own duties, so I couldn't get any sympathy . . . .[17]

The Germans zeroed in on Kerchner's men with machine gun fire. Sgt. Francis J. Pacyga was hit in the arm; a bullet struck Pfc. Lester W. Harris in the leg, and Pfc. William Cruz got clobbered in the leg and arm; they survived their injuries. With only a pistol for protection, Kerchner felt pretty helpless. The lieutenant picked up Harris' discarded weapon, and directed Cruz, who was only slightly wounded, to drag the other injured men closer to the cliff and stay with them. Kerchner then left the group.

Dodging enemy fire, the rest of the men began climbing the ropes, grabbing any free line to scale the cliffs. Lieutenant Kerchner ran down the beach looking for Lieutenant Colonel Rudder.[18] About 25-50 yards up the beach he found the commander and informed him about Captain Slater's boat going down, and that he [Kerchner] was assuming command over D Company. Rudder looked at the lieutenant and yelled, "get the hell out of there and get up and climb [a] rope." Kerchner, therefore, took up a rope and began moving up the precipice.

. . . Climbing the cliff was very easy, especially after training on these cliffs that we had worked on over in England. The shelling from the war ships and the bomb damage had hit the edge of the cliff and caused some dirt and large [amounts] of clay and shale to fall down so that you could almost walk part way up the cliff. The first 25 feet of it really didn't entail any climbing to any extent. The cliffs were about one hundred feet high at this point. I went up a smooth rope . . . .[19]

In only 15 minutes most of Kerchner's boat team had reached the top.

* * * *

LCA 887: Lt. Robert C. Arman, Company F

With the two D Company crafts landing off course, F Company's three LCAs were forced to beach further eastward than originally planned. Just before grounding to a halt, LCA 887 fired its two forward rockets. The plain rope carried over, but the other one fell short. Lt. Robert C. Arman led this boat team and ordered the other rockets to be carried to shore.

A **view of the huge shell craters created by the Allied bombers. Many Rangers fell into these deep pits and almost drowned. Photo taken on June 7, '44. Signal Corps Coll., USAMHI.**

Hauling in the rockets and ropes took time. They were extremely heavy. All the while Germans sprayed the area with rifle and machine gun fire. Grenades rained down on the Rangers, but they successfully set up the rockets and fired them. The ropes caught at the top, and Lieutenant Arman's boat team scaled the cliffs.

Sgt. William "L-Rod" Petty, the brashest Ranger in F Company, attempted to climb up one of the plain ropes, but the rope was wet and the cliff face too slippery. Sergeant Petty then tried a rope ladder. When he was about 30 feet up, the grapnel came loose, and Petty slid back down. Capt. Walter Block, the battalion surgeon, saw the sergeant fall. Petty and his B.A.R. were wet and muddy. Block said to him, "Soldier, get up that rope to the top of the cliff." Sergeant Petty could not contain his frustration and anger and snapped back, "I've been trying to get up this goddamn rope for five minutes, and if you think you can do any better you can f—ing well do it yourself." Captain Block turned away and dropped the subject.[20]

Meanwhile, Petty looked over and saw T/5 Carl Winsch climbing another rope ladder. Winsch made it to the top so Sergeant Petty quickly followed him. The two F Company Rangers were joined by Sgt. William M. McHugh, Pfc. Garness L. Colden and Pfc. William H. Coldsmith. The five Rangers headed out to their objective.

* * * *

LCA 884: Lt. Jacob J. Hill, Company F

LCA 884 slid in to the left of LCA 887. Lt. Jacob J. Hill's Company F team endured horrendous fire from the German infantry. Hill's men had replied with their small arms and B.A.R.s. The Germans continued firing as they ran for cover. The bullets struck against the men like hail as all their rockets were fired. Only four carried over the top. The craft ground to a halt right in front of a shell hole; the ramp went down and the men out front jumped into water shoulder-high. Three Rangers went down, wounded by enemy fire from their left flank. Lieutenant Hill remarked, "Those crazy sons of bitches are using live ammunition."[21]

Hill's men reached their ropes and found that they were wet and muddy and all the ropes were out in the open. One Ranger tried to scale the cliff free-style, but came sliding down. Stranded, Lieutenant Hill ran his boat team over to LCA 883's ropes and climbed them.

* * * *

LCA 883: Capt. Otto Masny, Company F

The last boat in the convoy, and the last to reach shore, was LCA 883. Capt. Otto "Big Stoop" Masny led LCA 883. They were about 100 yards west of their planned landing point, but Masny had spotted a jut in the cliff which provided cover from the flanking machine gun fire. Masny also observed that some of the other LCA ropes were being fired too soon and falling short. T/5 Herman Stein saw these ropes miss and thought they would all be stranded on the shore below the Pointe.

Captain Masny yelled to the British sailor piloting the LCA, "Don't fire those things until I give the word! We've got plenty of time!" To assure that Masny's orders would be followed, Lt. Richard A. Wintz pulled out his pistol and pointed it at the sailor. In no uncertain terms Lieutenant Wintz said to him, "You drop those gates or let those charges go before I give the order and I'll put a bullet in your head."[22] The frightened British sailor continued to head for shore and follow the other vessels.

Lt. G. K. Hodenfield, the *Stars and Stripes* journalist, accompanied Masny's Rangers.

> . . . When the nose of our LCA grounded against the sand, we stopped; he gave the word, and with a loud roar and whooshing sound, our rockets sailed over the top of the cliffs.
> . . . I had ducked my head when the first series of rockets exploded, heeding Masny's warning that we could be blinded if we looked at the rockets being fired, but then I looked up to see what had happened. I was lost in admiration of the pretty picture the rockets were making when the second and third series went off. The explosions were so startling that I fell over backward into the bottom of the boat, but as I rose shamefacedly, Masny patted me on the back and said, "If that scared you what do you think it did to the Germans?"[23]

The ramp went down. Pfc. Bill Walsh, Jr. recalled Captain Masny shouting,

> . . . "Go!" We all disembarked, dry head to foot. T/5 Bill L. Thompson and I headed for a shell hole to commence firing our 60mm mortar. We got off 4 shells before the incoming tide forced

us out to head for the cliffs. An enemy machine-gunner was to our left some yards distant, on a protrusion at the cliff top. I could see the narrow beach being churned up from his parallel fire. My forward motion couldn't escape his accuracy.[24]

    A bullet struck Walsh in the neck, and he crawled over to a medic who dressed his wound and saved his life. Sgt. Leon H. Otto was wounded at the same time. To ease his suffering they laid him on a pile of discarded life preservers and administered morphine. Otto was later taken back to the *Texas* and died on the operating table.[25]

    Sgt. Frank South was one of Capt. Walter "Doc" Block's medics. Just as South reached the shore he heard, "Medic!" shouted. Sergeant South remembered his first moments on the beach:

> . . . Immediately, there was the first call of 'Medic!' My regular aid kit was still attached to my pistol belt. Opening it, as I dodged the fire from the cliff, I reached the fallen Ranger with a chest wound. I was able to drag him to an indentation in the cliff face and begin to help him. The call 'Medic' was now repeated time after time. For awhile it seemed as if I was the only one retrieving and working on the wounded. Block and another medic had worked their way up to the cliff base and were beginning to treat men as fast as they could but it was not possible to set up a proper aid station on the beach . . . I worked along the entire beach, covering all three companies. Block devoted most of his attention to the most critically wounded.[26]

South set up a make-shift aid station down on the beach where Walsh and many other wounded Rangers lay, some writhing in their last battle — with death itself.

Pvt. Bill Walsh, Jr. Company F, 2d Rangers, severely wounded in the neck, but survived. Walsh Collection

As the injured waited to be evacuated other F Company Rangers zig-zagged their way to the base of the cliff. Sgt. Robert Youso and Pvt. Alvin White had already started up the ladders; at the bottom other Rangers anxiously awaited their turn. Captain Masny remained at the bottom and yelled advice and encouragement to his men.[27]

T/5 Herman Stein, F Company, climbed about half-way up the bluff when he felt like he was being pushed away from the rock. He struggled to continue his climb and then realized he was still wearing his Mae West, and it had inflated. Stein quickly tore it off. He looked up and saw Pfc. Raymond A. Cole just ahead of him; Cole slithered over the top followed by Sergeant Youso. The sergeant then yelled down to Stein, "Cole's been hit! Hit the dirt." Stein reached the top and stayed low. He saw Cole lying still, his eyes glazed over by death's veil. Youso and Stein waited for Sgt. Jack Richards to come up, and then the three took off.[28]

Lieutenant Wintz, in the same boat team as Youso and Stein, took up a plain rope. He was very tired. To compound his problems the rope was wet and muddy, and the slippery clay did not allow him to get a good foothold. When Wintz finally reached the top he located six other Rangers, and the squad started out immediately toward their objective on the left flank of the battalion's front.[29]

* * * *

Location: Base of cliff

At the base of the precipice Hodenfield waited nearly an hour before he reached the top. Journalists and photographers were not needed on the battlefield yet. To pass the time, Hodenfield lit a cigarette and thought to himself, "This is a helluva way to invade France." He sat and waited and smoked another cigarette.[30] While there he observed army photographer Lt. Amos Potts, who was

> fuming mad because here he was, in the middle of the greatest picture story of his life, and all his equipment had been water-soaked in the landing. He and I were too nervous to sit still, so we started digging some ammunition out of the sand where it already was being partially buried by the incoming tide.[31]

* * * *

DUKWS: Location: Off shore

As Hodenfield and Potts vented their frustrations, two of the three DUKWs approached the beach. Unlike the LCAs, with their flat bottoms, the DUKWs could not ground to shore due to the craters. One of the amphibious trucks floated close by. The men raised its extension ladder; it rested on the cliff at a terrible angle, and the waves rocked it rendering the ladder useless.

Another truck pulled its ladder up 80 feet into the air. Sgt. William Stivison climbed the ladder and fired the twin Lewis guns. The truck bobbed in the water and the ladder swayed from side-to-side. Stivison's accuracy was off, but the Germans zeroed in on his vulnerable position; tracers could be seen flying passed him.

Miraculously, Sergeant Stivison survived.[32]

* * * *

From the time the nine LCAs landed to the point at which the majority of the Rangers reached the top of the bluff, only 15 minutes had passed. It was only 7:30 a.m., and the small battalion had been reduced to less than 200 men. They lost two LCAs and one DUKW during the approach, and more than 20 Rangers had been killed or wounded when they hit the beach.

But Rudder's Rangers had breached Hitler's great Atlantic Wall. They now turned their attention to finding and destroying the 155mm guns, cutting German communications lines and setting up roadblocks, and holding their position until reinforcements arrived. It would not be an easy task.

Notes to Chapter 9

[1] Lane, 81.
[2] *Ibid.*, 81.
[3] Eikner, 11.
[4] Lane, 83-84.
[5] *Ibid.*
[6] Chapelie, Lisko's testimony, 136.
[7] Lane, 85.
[8] Eikner, 11.
[9] Eikner, 12.
[10] Telephone conversation with James Eikner, July 25, 1999.
[11] Ambrose, 408.
[12] Lane, 86-87.
[13] Leonard Lomell, Oral History, 6.
[14] Ambrose, 409.
[15] Lomell, notes to the author, July 27, 1999.
[16] Kerchner, 14.
[17] *Ibid.*, 15.
[18] George Kerchner's diary from D-Day to D+12, page 2. In possession of author, August 21, 1999.
[19] *Ibid.*, 16.
[20] Lane, 88 and Ambrose, 409.
[21] Lane, 89.
[22] *Ibid.*
[23] Chapelie, Hodenfield's testimony, 161-162.
[24] Bill Walsh, Jr., letter to the author, January 13, 1999.
[25] *Ibid.*
[26] Frank South, Oral History. See also, Astor, 180, and Ambrose, 410.
[27] Astor, 162.
[28] Herman Stein's account of the battle, transcript in possession of the author, June 17, 1999.
[29] *Ibid.*
[30] Chapelie, Hodenfield's testimony, 162.
[31] *Ibid.*
[32] Lane, 91.

Chapter 10

"Where 'n Hell Are They?":
The Battle for the Pointe

Unit: Headquarters
Location: On the cliff in the Command Post
With most of the men up and the mission proceeding, Lieutenant Colonel Rudder set up his command post in a large shell hole right on the edge of the bluff around 7:30 a.m. This hole was open toward the sea and offered some protection on the landward side. It had been formed against a large bunker of reinforced concrete.[1]

* * * *

Unit: Headquarters Company
Location: Down on the beach
Meanwhile, Communications Cpl. Lou Lisko and his comrades still down on the beach looked for Lieutenant Eikner. They needed to inform him that their radio was not working. Lisko described his search:

> . . . As I started to move along in order to find our lieutenant, the machine gun and rifleman on the left flank started to fire at me. First I thought I saw pebbles but in fact they were bullets. When I realized this I ran faster — and jumped into a crevice. Then, I saw Lieutenant Eikner . . . he was there with his carbine, and he already had twelve German prisoners . . . I told him about the situation. 'O.K., O.K., he said, you stay here with me and help me watch these German prisoners.'[2]

Photo taken in August 1944 by G. K. Hodenfield
Lisko's Ranger Box, USAMHI.

Location: Medic Station

Captain "Doc" Block continued to perform triage in the command post, out in the open. Block and his medics were kept very busy. They had already treated British commando Trevor and more wounded Rangers groped their way back to Headquarters. The medics and Doc Block would not get any rest for several days.

* * * *

Unit: Company E
Location: Center Of Line

As Dr. Block cared for the injured and the Headquarters Rangers tried to get their radios working while defending themselves against harassing German riflemen, other Americans attempted to carry out their individual missions. Company E was divided into four sections. The first group's task was to destroy the No. 3 German gun and its casemate.

Section two's mission was to push through the enemy position until it reached the main east-west highway and set up a defensive perimeter to prevent German reinforcements from getting through. Company E's third section was to destroy the concrete observation post which provided the firing coordinates for all six guns. Group four was to assist the third section and then, if necessary, help the second section near the highway.

* * * *

Unit: Company F
Location: Left Flank

F Company deployed on the left flank. They were to take out the Nos. 1 and 2 gun positions and the machine gun nest in the side of the cliff to the east.

* * * *

Unit: Company D
Location: Extreme Right Flank (west)

Company D's men were to take the guns out on the right flank: positions 4, 5, and 6. The original plans stated once the guns and emplacements were destroyed they would cut the German communications and assemble at a line about 300 yards inland near the southwest edge of the German-occupied area.

* * * *

At the inland position, Companies D and F and part of E Company would head toward the coastal highway where a section of Company E was to be waiting as originally planned. After their rendezvous, the Rangers would establish a roadblock at the black-top road and stop any German reinforcements coming from the Grandcamp area.[3]

While the Ranger battalion had taken casualties during their assault on the

Pointe, they had fared better than expected. Their real shock came when they found that the big guns were not in place; prior to D-Day they had been hidden away at an alternate position. The only thing the men saw in the casemates were telephone poles which from the air had looked like gun barrels. As disciplined soldiers they remained focused. They would continue inland, set up roadblocks, cut the German communications, keep searching for the Pointe-du-Hoc battery and render it inoperable.

* * * *

Unit: S/Sgt. Jack Kuhn, Company D, 2d Platoon
Location: Heading toward the black-top highway
Topping the bluff, S/Sgt. Jack Kuhn, D Company, was briefly separated from his boat team and alone. As he neared an exit road from the Pointe he spotted Pfc. Jack Conaboy, 2d Platoon, D Company's first scout. The two men ran from a shell hole to the exit road; a sniper zeroed in. A bullet went through Conaboy's canteen and nailed him in his behind. Kuhn asked if he was all right, and Conaboy verified that he was okay. The staff sergeant looked around and about ten yards from his position he spied a column from second platoon, D Company. 1st Sgt. Len Lomell led the group.

* * * *

Unit: 1st Sgt. Leonard Lomell, acting platoon commander, Company D, 2d Platoon
Location: Heading out toward the black top highway
Unlike most of the boat teams, Lomell's group remained intact and fought as a single unit throughout the battle for the Pointe. After successfully climbing the cliff, Lomell and his group of 22 Rangers first came upon Capt. Sammy Baugh, E Company.

Captain Baugh had been severely wounded when a bullet passed through the back of his hand and into the magazine which had then exploded, blowing his hand apart. Sergeant Lomell told him, "Hey, Captain, we'll send you back a medic."

Lomell's 2d Platoon then speedily advanced toward his unit's main objective, Nos. 4, 5, and 6 gun positions.[4] Running from shell crater to shell crater they rushed to the gun emplacements. The 2d Platoon was the first Ranger contingency to see that the guns were not in their supposed location; they saw only the telephone poles. "Where could they have gone?" Lomell reasoned that the Germans had moved them to a safer position inland. As evidence, he noted tracks and other markings coming from the casemates.

The D Company Rangers thought they'd soon hear the "boom" of the big guns, but no such sound came, only rifle, machine gun, anti-aircraft and artillery fire. With no guns at the Pointe, 1st Sgt. Leonard Lomell led his platoon toward the exit road. They weren't abandoning their search for the guns; they were simply heading for their second assignment — setting up a roadblock at the black-top highway on the west flank.

Near the exit road a German machine-gunner raked the 2d Platoon. T/5

The Liberation of Pointe du Hoc

Vaughan fell mortally wounded; Lomell and his men dove for cover. Without hesitation, several Rangers lobbed grenades toward the enemy position; a loud explosion occurred and the gun position fell silent.

1st Sergeant Lomell peered over the lip of the hole; he observed Kuhn and saw that Pfc. Conaboy had been hit. "Can you move?" Lomell yelled over to Conaboy.

The private shouted an affirmative. The sergeant then replied, "Then get the hell over here!" Kuhn helped Conaboy as the private quickly hobbled to Lomell's position.

Where ya' wounded?" Len asked. Embarrassed the private answered, "In the rear."

Len ordered Conaboy to drop his pants and, within seconds, Kuhn and Lomell had extracted the projectile; they gave the prize to Pfc. Conaboy.[5]

Only minutes had passed. 1st Sergeant Lomell and his 2d Platoon immediately resumed their advance — charging as fast as they could and running through the German bunkers and along the crater-pocked ground. At any given moment assailants appeared out of underground tunnels, and they were reminded that the enemy still occupied much of the area. Lomell described the intense fighting:

> . . . half a dozen of them would pop out of an underground tunnel .
> . . we'd drive them out and fight them and they'd run like rabbits,
> you know, right into their holes, and out they went. But we never
> stopped. We kept firing and charging all the way through their
> buildings area, where they came out of their billets in all states of
> undress. We were confronted with them there on our way up the
> road from the Pointe to the coast road.[6]

Photo takenfrom a postcard
Lisko's Ranger Box, USAMHI

'

Unit: Company D, 1ˢᵗ Platoon
Location: Extreme Right flank

While Lomell's 2d Platoon rapidly proceeded inland, Lieutenant Kerchner, who came in on LCA 858, had topped the bluff and headed for the three gun positions — Nos. 4, 5, and 6. As he zig-zagged along the war-torn terrain he saw fellow D Company men — Sgt. Michael J. Branley, T/5 Clarence J. Long and Pfc. Melvin C. Hoffelbower, Jr., trying to locate the sniper and machine gun fire.

It was difficult to see either friend or foe because hundreds of huge craters had been created by the severe naval and air bombardment. Many of the soldiers had automatically used these holes to shelter themselves from the enemy fusillade, but at the same time this hindered the officers from locating and organizing their units.

Kerchner soon picked up more men from his company — T/Sgt. Richard Spleen, Pfc. Robert Carty, Sgt. Richard McLaughlin, Pfc. Leonard Rubin, S/Sgt. Joseph Flanagan, T/5 Harvey Huff and Sgt Morris Webb. The squad soon attracted German artillery and machine gun fire. "Being the first time I was under artillery fire . . . this was a rather terrifying experience," Kerchner later remarked. Bullets and debris flew about them like hailstones, but the Rangers kept advancing; they felt safer on the move.

When the lieutenant and his men got nearer to the gun casemates they sighted a 40mm anti-aircraft gun deployed to the west. Kerchner and the men dove into a shell crater full of Rangers. The lieutenant directed Huff to fire at the gun. T/5 Harvey Huff took three quick shots, but missed each time.

While in the crater a sergeant jumped in and informed the D Company men that the big gun casemates were empty; Lieutenant Kerchner directed the men to proceed immediately to their second mission, establishing a roadblock. No one argued, the German gunners at the anti-aircraft gun were firing for affect at the group; his men took off, but Kerchner remained in the hole.[7] He continued an attempt to knock out the 40mm gun, but the fire from the enemy position was so thick he could not get a shot off. He soon gave up and quietly crawled away. It was nearly 7:30 a.m.

In order to more safely traverse the area, the lieutenant jumped into a German communications trench. It was deep and zig-zagged across the battle zone. Alone, Kerchner carefully crept down the communication lane. "I was by myself at this time, and I never felt so lonesome before or since in all my life because every time I came to a corner of this communications trench, where I had to make a turn to see what was in the next 25 yard section, I didn't know whether I was going to come face to face with a German or not."

His imagination began to get the better of him: maybe he was going to be captured; maybe he was surrounded and had no chance. Kerchner had to rejoin his men. It felt a lot safer within a group than on one's own. The trench line ran for about 150 yards and then came out near the ruins of a French farm house.[8]

Near the farmhouse Kerchner saw his first American casualty. He described the scene:

> . . . There was a German machine gun in this road leading out from
> the Pointe, and I came up there and I saw the first one of my men
> who was wounded, a boy named Vaughan, a T/5 machine gunner,

a real wonderful young fellow. I realized as soon as I saw him that he was dying. He had been practically stitched across with a machine gun. He wasn't in any pain because he was hit too bad. I know he knew that he was dying, and all I could tell him was, Bill, we'll send the medic to look after you. There wasn't any point in me staying there with him: there wasn't anything I could do for him, and I felt that the best thing for me to do was to get up the road to where the rest [of D Company was deployed].[9]

Kerchner left Vaughan and continued toward the highway.

* * * *

As the Ranger squads advanced farther inland they began to meet stronger resistance. The Germans had created a fortified perimeter about three miles inland from the Pointe. This line included mine-fields, barbed wire, and machine gun emplacements. The fortifications had been constructed to defend against an attack from the land, but now the Germans made a 180 degree turn in order to meet the 2d Ranger Battalion coming like Titans up from the sea.

* * * *

Unit: Company F
Location: Left flank

Elements of Company F were encountering experiences similar to that of Kerchner's and Lomell's platoons. Sgt. William "L-Rod" Petty, T/5 Carl Winsch, Sgt. William McHugh, Pfc. Garness L. Colden and Pfc. William H. Coldsmith crawled and crept from shell hole to shell hole toward their objective — gun position No. 2. From a distance they saw the gun emplacement was completely destroyed. Sergeant Petty remained focused and led the group to their second goal, one of the exit roads. When they neared the German fortified area inland, Lieutenant Arman's F Company group joined up with Petty's squad.

The F Company boys carefully moved through the minefield and barbed wire. Most of the area was completely pocked with shell holes; with hundreds of craters, the entire Pointe looked like the surface of the moon. The mines had either been buried or detonated by the intense bombardment. Mortar fire, however, began to fall among the Rangers. The group advanced south watching and covering their movement. Near the ruins of a farm, Arman's group encountered 1st Sgt. Robert W. Lang and three other E Company Rangers.

* * * *

Unit: Company E
Location: Advancing inland

Sergeant Lang and the other E Company men had landed with Rudder. After climbing up the cliff, Lang took the group toward the No. 3 gun position. They inched close to the casemate only to find a pile of broken steel and crumbled concrete.

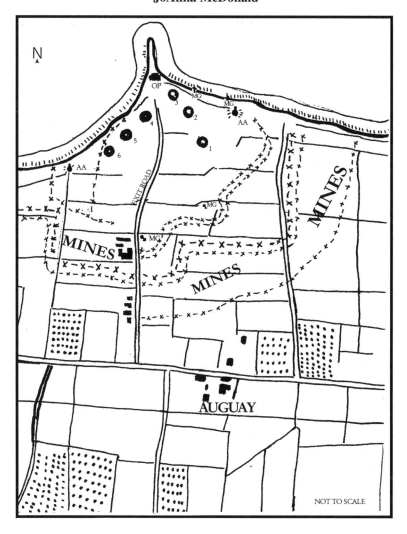

Map 5
German defensive line inland.
Fields of land mines, barbed wire, machine gun emplacements, and an intricate system of
trenches and tunnels protected the Pointe from a land attack.

One of the Rangers thought the Army Air Corps and Navy bombardment had totally wiped out the gun. But Sergeant Lang noted that no gun had been here during the bombardment. He saw broken and scattered pieces of telephone poles sticking out of the casemate and realized what had happened.[10]

Like the other Ranger squads, they turned to their second mission, the black-top highway and establishing a roadblock. As they headed out, artillery or mortar rounds exploded nearby. Sergeant Lang stopped briefly to radio back to the fire support group at Rudder's Headquarters. The sergeant wanted to inform HQ that he was moving his men inland and that they should relay to the American mortar crews and the Navy to lift any firing in his sector.

The Liberation of Pointe du Hoc

While Lang attempted to call the command post his men continued advancing. Not able to reach anyone on the radio, Sergeant Lang realized that the artillery fire now separated him from his men. The sergeant moved into a field and bumped into three other E Company Rangers. Shortly after, Lang and his new squad ran into Lieutenant Arman's Company F group.

* * * *

Photo of broken telephone poles. After the German's pulled their guns away from the Pointe they replaced them with telephone poles to fool Allied Intelligence. Lisko's Ranger Box, USAMHI

Unit: E & F Companies
Location: Left Flank going inland toward AuGuay

The make-shift unit proceeded down the lane. Sergeant Petty fanned out to the left and crossed several fields and neared a chateau. Seeing no Germans, he rejoined the group. The Rangers reached the lane that intersected with the black-top highway. This was the area where they were to setup a blockade.

Once on the road they turned west toward Grandcamp, and slowly moved to the small village of AuGuay. A German machine gunner watched the group. When they were within 100 yards he let loose. Rangers dove into the brush and scattered. Sergeant Petty and Sgt. William H. McHugh, along with another unnamed Ranger, separated from the squad and crept toward the area where they believed the enemy machine-gunner to be.

Two other Germans miraculously appeared; Petty hit the dirt firing his B.A.R. at the same time. Petty's bullets whizzed by the German soldiers just missing them. They raised their hands and yelled, "*Kamerad*! *Kamerad*!"

The frustrated and excited Americans accepted the Germans' surrender. Petty was amazed that he had missed those "sons of bitches," and wanted to know where they had come from. Upon investigation, Petty found a deep shelter hole which was well camouflaged. It was disconcerting to realize that the enemy could appear at any time from anywhere.

Escorting their two prisoners, the patrol entered AuGuay but found no Germans. The cagey adversary had disappeared. Cautiously, the F Company squad moved to the west side of the village. There they anxiously waited for other men from E and F Companies to join them.[11]

* * * *

Unit: Company F
Location: Left flank at the cliff going inland
Near the coast, other F Company Rangers attempted to take out a German machine gun emplacement which was sending a deadly sweeping cross-fire on the Americans down on the beach. LCA 884 and LCA 883 had landed on the extreme left of the line. Pfc. William E. Anderson, from LCA 884, met up with two fellow F Company Rangers. The three spied the German position to their east.

The Rangers snuck along the edge of the bluff behind a hedgerow. When they reached within 100 yards of the position, they could not pinpoint the automatic weapon. "Where 'n hell are they?" Anderson angrily questioned. None of the men could sight the nest. The Rangers realized the Germans were probably nestled in just below the cliff top, and there was an overhang above the enemy's position. It was well protected. Anderson realized there was no way the three could take out the weapon. One of them suggested they get out of there. They all agreed and did an about-face and headed back to where they had started from.

Anderson became separated from the group and met two other Company F men, Pfc. John Bacho and S/Sgt. James E. Fulton. The three headed south toward the black-top road. Using leap frog tactics to advance, the three Rangers made steady progress. The Germans were everywhere and well hidden. When Anderson, Bacho, and Fulton had gone about 100 yards, they bumped into three more F Company Rangers. Lt. Jacob J. Hill was among the group.

Hill took command of the small squad, and they continued south. For the time being no Germans showed themselves; only occasional sniper fire was heard. The six men came to a hedgerow which ran east-west. Hill and three soldiers turned west; Fulton and Bacho continued through the hedgerow in order to cover their flank. But the two Rangers advanced too far south and were separated from the group. Sergeants Fulton and Bacho soon arrived at the black-top highway and joined up with Lieutenant Arman's F Company unit.[12]

* * * *

Unit: Company F
Location: Heading inland
Lieutenant Hill's party of four, meanwhile, continued west; they saw a lane with hedgerows on both sides. Looking to their right they saw a German in the field; the soldier spotted the Americans as well and immediately surrendered. The Rangers' attention was then turned to the sound of a machine gun near the exit road. Lieutenant

Hill determined to take the enemy soldier with them as they attacked the German machine gun nest.

Weaving their way through a shell-cratered wheatfield, the men hurried toward the road; a burst of automatic fire was heard again, and they dove for cover. Hill's group soon realized they had not been sighted; the enemy gunner blazed away at fellow Rangers. The young lieutenant directed two men of his group to guard the prisoner, and with Pfc. Anderson, Hill inched to within 25 yards of the machine gun. The two hid in a low embankment.

To Anderson's surprise, Lieutenant Hill stood straight up to get a better look at the German location. At the same time, Hill yelled out, "You bastard sons of bitches, you couldn't hit a bull in the ass with a bass fiddle." Hearing an American behind them, the Germans swung their weapon around; Hill dropped down as bullets flew over head. He could feel the projectiles cut through the air. Anderson gently tossed the lieutenant a grenade; Hill pulled the pin and hurled it. "Boom," the grenade hit its mark, and the German firing stopped.[13]

* * * *

Unit: Company F
Location: Near the cliff
As Hill and Anderson took out the machine gun emplacement inland, other German positions near the crest continued to elude the Rangers. Lt. Richard Wintz's F Company group was organized after Pfc. Anderson decided not to assault the machine gun nestled just below the edge of the cliff. This same gunner now harassed Wintz's men. T/5 Herman Stein was with this group.

Stein teamed up with Jack Richards, a B.A.R. man, once they had both topped the bluff. As the assistant to the B.A.R. man, Stein carried 200 extra rounds of ammunition which was burdensome. The steady bursts of machine gun fire slowed the party, but the Germans withdrew to a more favorable position.

With the enemy fire subsiding a bit, Wintz set up a defensive line on the far left flank. The machine gun fire, however, resumed farther out. "We exchanged fire and picked up sight of machine gun bursts coming from an opening in the hedge row some one hundred yards out," Stein later recalled.[14] Wintz's men could not take out the German gunner. The lieutenant, therefore, relayed the message back to Rudder's command post.

* * * *

Unit: Headquarters
Location: Moving out toward the left flank near the cliff perimeter
Lieutenant Colonel Rudder received word from Lieutenant Wintz and directed Lieutenant Vermeer, the engineer, to eliminate the gun. Vermeer took several men with him and set out on the mission:

> . . . We moved through the shell craters and had just reached the
> open ground where the machine gun could cover us also when we
> ran into a patrol from F Company on the same mission. Once we

ran out of shell holes and could see nothing but flat 200-300 yards of open ground in front of us, I was overwhelmed with the sense that it would be impossible to reach our objective without heavy losses.[15]

Before Vermeer's squad could launch their attack, they received orders from Rudder to return to the command post.

* * * *

Unit: Headquarters
Location: Command Post near the cliff

The colonel had brought along Navy Lt. Kenneth Norton and Army Capt. Jonathan Harwood as a shore fire control party. Just before they signaled the coordinates of the enemy machine gun emplacement to the ships, a Navy shell hit the side of a bunker where Harwood, Norton and Rudder were working. Lieutenant Colonel Rudder was wounded in the right arm and later remembered the horrifying scene. "The artillery captain . . . a nice-looking, black haired boy . . . was killed right here. The Navy lieutenant, who was spotting with us, fell right here. It knocked me over . . . ."[16]

Vermeer witnessed the explosion from his position:

> . . . The hit turned the men completely yellow. It was as though they had been stricken with jaundice. It wasn't only their faces and hands, but the skin beneath their clothes and the clothes which were yellow from the smoke of that shell — it was probably a colored marker shell.[17]

Corporal Lisko stationed in the command post recalled that a "ranger came rolling into the Command Post, yelling: 'Rudder's hit again, Rudder's hit again!'" Lisko explained what had happened:

> . . . A shell from Battleship *Texas* landed and hit the bunker where Colonel Rudder was. It was an ironic situation: a man from Texas wounded by his own battleship. Doctor Block, who was taking care of some wounded rangers in the command post, took his first aid equipment and went out. Immediately, the left flank machine gun fired at him. He ducked down really quick, and looked at me. A medic and I went out and ran across the bomb crater to the other side, firing in the direction of the Germans to give him cover. But the German did not fire back. The doctor finally reached Colonel Rudder and gave him a bandage treatment.[18]

With the shore fire control party dead, the colonel told Lieutenant Eikner to try and reach the destroyer *Satterlee* and have her big guns take out the destructive German machine-gunner perched on the east side of the cliff.

Assuming that communications might be cut from the big ships out in the Channel, Eikner had brought along an antiquated signal lamp. As presumed, none of the radios could reach the Naval armada so the lieutenant set up the lamp. He flicked the light on and off and relayed the message and coordinates of the German position.

In addition to the *Satterlee,* Eikner contacted another ship and asked them to come in and pick up some of the seriously injured men. Under fire, the Navy brought in a small craft and evacuated a few of the wounded.[19] Eikner explained:

> ... There we were with no naval contact and the enemy was attacking all the time and we needed desperately the fire support from the Navy. We had brought in with us, or at least loaded up on the boats a couple of old WWI type signal lamps. Fortunately we had trained our boys in the techniques of using international morse code on the signal lamps with the idea that we may just have need of this during the invasion ... We lost one of the lamps out at sea, but I inquired of my radio man if we had managed to get in one of the signal lamps. He said, ' Yes, there is one down under the cliff,' and he went down to get it, under fire. It was brought up, and it was tripod mounted. We set it upright in the middle of the shell hole command post, and we found enough dry cell batteries to get it going ... We immediately put the lamp into use and established communications that way.[20]

Lt. Col. James Rudder in his command post, June 8, '44.
Note signal lamp set up behind him. The Rangers used this lamp to communicate with the Navy battleships and destroyers. Cpl. Louis Lisko, Lieutenant Eikner and other communications personnel operated the lamp. Lisko's Ranger Box, USAMHI

This signal lamp, of World War 1 vintage, was used by the Rangers at Pointe du Hoc on D-Day to call down and direct naval gunfire against the enemy. At the time, this was critical for the survival of the Ranger operation.

At mid-morning on D-Day shell fire knocked out the Naval Shore Fire Control Party and communications with the Navy was lost. This was at a time when the enemy was pressing in to push us back into the sea, and the Navy was our only source of supporting fire. First Lt. James W. Eikner then had this lamp erected in a defilade position within the cliffside Command Post and immediately continued to direct fire against the enemy. The lamp was also operated by T/Sgt Jack Roach, T/4 Charles Parker, T/5 Steve Liscinski and T/5 Lou Lisko.

Communications with the Navy was a textbook example of the best of ship-to-shore operations. Probably, this was the first time in military history that a signal lamp, utilizing Morse Code, was used to direct naval gunfire.

Later in the day, radio communications was resumed with the Navy, but the lamp was still used as a backup and for flagging down passing ships seeking aid in evacuating wounded and prisoners and bringing in supplies.

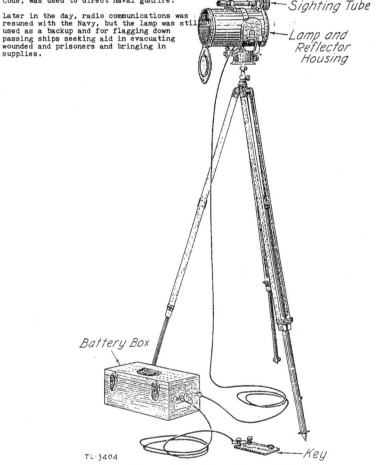

Sighting Tube

Lamp and Reflector Housing

Battery Box

TL-3404   *Key*

FIGURE 23.—Signal lamp EE-84.

A diagram of a signal lamp similar to the one Eikner used on the Pointe. **Eikner, T/4 Charles Parker, T/5 Steven Liscinsky and Cpl. Lou Lisko worked the lamp through June 6-7. The men communicated with the Navy ships, and in turn, the battleships and destroyers sent in covering fire to destroy several German positions. Eikner bluntly stated, "The Navy saved our butts." Eikner Coll.**

Unit: Company F
Location: Left Flank of cliff perimeter

The *Satterlee* approached the coast and opened up on the German position. T/5 Stein and his comrades anxiously watched the powerful Navy guns. "It wasn't long before the first shell burst close by the gate. The next shell tore dead center into

The Liberation of Pointe du Hoc

the target. That's a lot better than assaulting it, we thought with some relief." Stein and other F Company men cheered when they saw the German emplacement blown off the cliff.[21]

With the German machine-gunner out of action, Stein and his buddy, Jack Richards decided to traverse the bomb-cratered fields. Along with other F Company Rangers they reconnoitered through the obstacles. No German fire had occurred for sometime, and the men seemed to relax. In defiance of the war, Jack perched himself at the top of one of the dirt piles. He scanned the horizon with his field glasses and gradually raised himself higher, gambling with death. "Hey, Herm, take a look, those are our guys way out there," Jack said.

Sure enough, slightly to the right and about three to four hundred yards out, the men thought they saw American helmets. Richards took back the glasses and checked again to confirm that they were Rangers. T/5 Herman Stein slipped back down into the crater and said, "Hey Jack, get down; there might be a sniper around."

Just then Stein heard a soft-thud; Jack fell forward over the edge of the shell crater. Herm caught Jack's ankles and pulled him into the hole. Herman Stein sadly recalled the death of his friend:

> . . . He was a short, powerhouse of a man, played college football, and respected by all. I admired and looked up to Jack as much as anyone in the outfit. In fact, before embarking he was told he didn't have to come, due to his high blood pressure. In training Jack would never have made a mistake and stayed so long under observation. There was a flap of skin about one and a half inches square, opened up on one side of his neck where the blood was just gushing out with every pump. I automatically sealed back the opening not realizing till later that was where the bullet had come out and not in. The thick red liquid leaked out relentlessly and for three weeks I carried Jack's blood on the lower arms of my winter undershirt . . . Jack's eyes opened glassily, and I knew he was gone.[22]

With no time to mourn for his friend, Herman took Jack's B.A.R. Another soldier, Sgt. Carl Bombardier, from Company F, came over to find out what had happened. He saw Jack Richards lying in a pool of blood.

Herman Stein looked at Sergeant Bombardier, who was nicknamed "Bomber"; "Hey, Bomber, I got to take the gun. Did you run into anybody from the 2nd section?" Stein asked.

Bomber answered, "Yeah, I just passed Cloise."

Cloise was of average height and slight build. Stein didn't think Pfc. Cloise Manning was the best choice to carry an extra ten clips of B.A.R. ammunition, but there wasn't time to search out a better candidate so T/5 Stein took Manning as his assistant.[23]

* * * *

Unit: Headquarters and Company D

—102—

Location: Near gun emplacements 3, 4, 5, 6 and German Anti-Aircraft gun

Sniper fire not only affected Stein's sector, but the men at Headquarters also found themselves a target even though they were stationed in a relatively safe area. A German set up near gun position No. 4 had calibrated the distance and peppered the command post.

Pfc. William Cruz, D Company, who had been slightly wounded and left behind to guard Headquarters, was ordered to find and take out the German rifleman. Along with T/5 Gerald A. Eberle, HQ Company, Cruz took off after him.

The German gunners on the west flank at their anti-aircraft gun position spotted the two Rangers and sent a volley of bullets toward the Americans. So thick and fast came the death-dealing missiles that Cruz and Eberle turned their attention to the 40mm gun. Ignoring the sniper, Cruz and Eberle were determined to destroy the anti-aircraft piece.

Zig-zagging from crater to crater, the two happened upon T/Sgt. Richard J. Spleen, D Company, and T/Sgt. Clifford E. Mains from Company E. Spleen, Mains, and about ten other Rangers in their group, were also planning to attack the gun. Sergeants Spleen and Mains held off their assault. German artillery shells fell around the area, and they did not want to expose their position to the battery.

What to do? They had to destroy the menacing gun, but the Germans might have a radio and call back artillery support. They talked it over: if they crawled close enough to the anti-aircraft gun location the Germans could not call down artillery on themselves.

Inching their way forward, Cruz and the others stopped; a German helmet protruded from a crater. The Rangers close to the object saw that a stick was used to display the helmet and thus they did not fire. Those further back, however, could not see that it was a ruse, and they blasted the invisible enemy.

German artillery and mortar fire immediately began to probe the area. Pfc. Cruz crept back to gun position No. 3; he hunkered down in a crater and looked around. He was alone. A gloomy solitude fell upon Cruz. Where did they all go? "Anybody there? Everybody all right? Okay?" Cruz shouted.

"Yeah, yeah, okay," Sergeant Mains replied. The German artillery continued for about a quarter of an hour. Pfc. Cruz started toward a collapsed trench; he caught a glimpse of Sergeant Spleen and two other men going around the corner of another trench. Small arms fire and the anti-aircraft gun erupted. The private clenched the earth. He then spotted Germans rushing by, but they did not see the lone American.

Another blast of rifle and machine gun fire resounded then suddenly fell silent. Pfc. Cruz waited for a bit, and finally went to investigate. He found G.I. guns stacked in a neat pile; no dead Americans lay near them nor were there any wounded. They had all disappeared.

Cruz had seen enough. The German sniper and anti-aircraft gun were still operational, but alone there was nothing he could accomplish. He returned to the command post as quickly as possible and recounted the disappearance of several comrades to Lieutenant Colonel Rudder. Intelligence reports had described elaborate underground tunnels on the Pointe. Cruz's story confirmed these accounts. Everyone would have to be on high alert. Enemy snipers could easily appear and vanish before the Rangers could even return fire.[24]

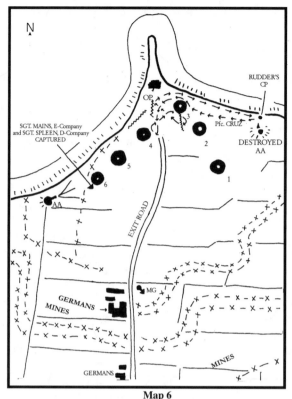

Map 6
Area where Pfc. Cruz, Sergeants Spleen and Mains fought.

Unit: Company E, Lieutenant Lapres' squad
Location: Cliff perimeter, German observation post, center of line

In the center of the line and toward the tip of the Pointe, two sections from E Company were to set up a defensive perimeter near the command post and capture German fortifications. But before this task was accomplished their mission instructed them to take out the Observation Post and gun position No. 3.

The first E Company Rangers from LCA 861 discovered that the concrete Observation Post was undamaged. Only about 20 feet away from the post, S/Sgt. Charles H. Denbo and Pvt. Harry W. Roberts crawled toward a trench in front of the formidable structure. The Germans carefully pointed their rifles and machine guns through the small slits in the Observation Post; a crash of rifle and machine gun blasts resounded. Bullets zipped and smacked dangerously close to the Americans.

Pinned down, the Company E Rangers threw four grenades toward the concrete bunker; three bounced through the slits. Muffled explosions echoed; the German machine gun fell silent, but Sergeant Denbo was hit by a rifle bullet. Lt. Theodore E. Lapres, Jr., Sgt. Andrew J. Yardley, T/Sgt. Harold W. Gunther and Pfc. William D. Bell, all from Company E, soon joined the battle.

"Get that bazooka over here. See if you can put a round through there!" Lapres yelled to Yardley. Sergeant Yardley took a deep breath, aimed his bazooka and fired. The round bounced off the firing slit and exploded. They reloaded and sent the second round right through the slit. The concrete post convulsed as another muted blast was heard.[25]

Lieutenant Lapres directed Yardley to cover him and the other men as they jumped up and sprinted around the right side of the Observation Post; no enemy fire came from the structure so Lapres' group moved inland to the black-top highway.[26]

* * * *

Unit: Company E, Lieutenant Leagans' squad
Location: Cliff perimeter, German Observation Post, center of line

Unknown to Lieutenant Lapres' squad, another group from E Company assaulted the Observation Post from the southeast. As Lt. Joseph E. Leagans, S/Sgt. Joseph J. Cleaves, Pfc. Victor J. Aguzzi, T/5 Leroy J. Thompson, and Pfc. Charles H. Bellows, Jr., started away from the cliff they saw a German soldier near the Observation Post dropping grenades down onto the beach. There were still Americans down there, and although Leagans' group was supposed to head straight for the main highway, they could not ignore this grenadier.

Pfc. Bellows crawled to the No. 3 gun position in order to provide cover fire while the other men inched closer to the German soldier. Once within range, Leagans' squad lobbed grenades. Four explosions resounded, but the grenadier escaped injury and retreated under the entrance to the Observation Post.

Lieutenant Leagans, Sergeant Cleaves, and T/5 Thompson tried to go around the bunker and attack it from the rear. Cleaves tripped a mine and was seriously wounded, but Leagans and Thompson inched closer to the outpost. Sergeant Thompson observed a radio antennae on the roof of the structure and promptly shot it away. Attempting to circle the building was not easy. After hurling a grenade through the front entrance, Leagans decided to move on. Other Rangers with demolition materials would have to take care of the OP.

* * * *

Unit: Company E
Location: Cliff perimeter, German Observation Post, center of line

While Lieutenant Leagans and Thompson headed for their original mission farther inland, the lieutenant directed Pfc. Aguzzi to stand watch over the entrance of the Observation Post. Seconds later Lapres' squad appeared from the rear of the building startling Aguzzi. Lapres told the private to stay put. Then Lapres moved out. Sergeant Yardley had stayed in another trench facing the embrasure.

Alone for only a short time, four more Rangers from LCA 861 soon joined Sergeant Yardley in the trench. Cpl. Paul L. Medeiros and Pfc. George W. Mackey were among the four soldiers. Seeing more Americans entering Yardley's trench, the Germans within the bunker resumed blasting that position.

There was no way of knowing how many Germans were left in this damn indestructible, bunker. Yardley certainly had no idea; he told the new arrivals that the building had been hit several times, but it seemed there was a infinite number of enemy soldiers who wouldn't give up.

Sergeant Yardley suggested to Corporal Medeiros that he (Medeiros) scale down the cliff and bring up some high explosives. They would blow the building off of the Pointe. The corporal, uneasy about the plan, took another look at the bunker. A German swung his gun around and opened up on Medeiros as he dove for cover. "I'll get it, but I don't see how we're gonna get close enough to use it. We can't get any covering fire on them," Corporal Medeiros pointed out to Yardley.[27]

Yardley rethought the idea and directed the three other Rangers to try and catch up with Lieutenant Lapres. The sergeant and Medeiros would provide covering fire for them. At the signal, Yardley and Medeiros let loose a fusillade of bazooka rounds and rifle blasts. The three Americans took off; a German hidden on the roof of the Observation Post fired at the group. Bullets tore through the Rangers; Mackey fell dead, but the other two escaped and headed inland.

For the rest of D-Day and through the night of June 7th, Sergeant Yardley and Corporal Medeiros kept guard on one side of the OP while Pfc. Aguzzi, deployed on the other side of the bunker, kept watch at the entrance. Neither party ever realized the other was there.[28]*

Although the OP was not immediately blown off the cliff, the E Company Rangers had knocked out the radio antennae. The Germans, therefore, could not call back firing coordinates to their artillery farther inland.

*The OP survived the intense heavy bombing and shelling and was finally cleaned out on the afternoon of D+1 when two satchel charges of C-2 were thrown in the entrance. Pvt. Aguzzi thought the Germans were finally wiped out but eight unharmed Germans came out of the OP with their hands up. The Americans never knew how many enemy soldiers were in the position because it was connected by underground tunnels.[29]

Notes to Chapter 10

[1] Eikner, 13.

[2] Chapelie, Lisko's testimony, 137-138.

[3] Lane 117-118.

[4] Lomell, 7.

[5] Interview with Len Lomell, August 21, 1999. Conaboy kept the bullet and put it on his dog tags. Months later the private was horrified when his chain broke while he was in the latrine. The bullet fell right into the toilet and was lost forever.

[6] *Ibid.*, 10.

[7] Kerchner, 19-20 and George Kerchner's diary, page 3.

[8] *Ibid.*

[9] *Ibid.*, 21.

[10] Historical Division. *Small Unit Actions: France: 2d Ranger Battalion at Pointe du Hoc, Saipan: 27th Division on Tanapag Plain, Italy: 351st Infantry at Santa Maria Infante, France: 4th Armored Division at Singling* (Washington, D.C.: War Department, 1946), 24-26.

[11] bid., 28-29.

[12] *Ibid.*, 29. See also Lane, 123-124.

[13] *Small Unit Action*, 29-30. Lane, 123-124.

[14] Herman Stein's account of the battle, transcript supplied by Herman Stein on June 17, 1999.

[15] Elmer Vermeer's oral history, Eisenhower Center.

[16] *Collier's* Magazine, June 11, 1954, 27.

[17] Vermeer's oral history. See also Ambrose, 414.

[18] Chapelie, Lisko's testimony, 140.

[19] *Ibid.*, 17.

[20] Eikner, 16.

[21] Stein.

[22] Herman Stein's account of the battle, transcript supplied by Herman Stein on June 17, 1999.
[23] *Ibid.*
[24] Cruz's story can be found in *Small Unit Actions*, 24-26.
[25] *Ibid.*, 22-23.
[26] *Ibid.*
[27] Lane, 119-120.
[28] *Small Unit Actions,* 23. Lane, 119-120.
[29] *Small Unit Actions,* 23. Lomell's notes to the author July 27, 1999.

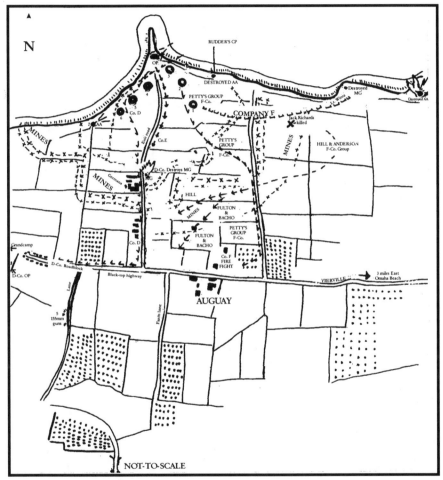

Map 7
Battle for the Pointe
Cos. D and E head inland on the right flank; patrols from Co. F advance on the left while other F Company men set up a defensive position near the Pointe. Rudder establishes his command post (CP) near the cliff; the German Observation Post was located at the very tip of the Pointe.

Chapter 11

"Here're the Goddamn Guns":
Silent Guns, Deadly Fire

Units: Companies D, E, and F
Location: Moving inland

It was about 7:45 a.m. Approximately forty-seven Rangers from Companies D, E, and F headed farther inland. Each unit advanced from various points across the mile front of the battalion, and each progressed at different speeds depending on the combat conditions the squad or unit fell up against.

* * * *

Unit: Company D, 2d Platoon
Location: Exit road going inland

Over on the far right (west flank) 1st Sgt. Len Lomell, D Company, and S/Sgt. Jack Kuhn on the exit road, split the 2d Platoon and made their way in two columns, one column on each side of the exit lane. Then Lomell and Kuhn carefully and quickly headed for the main highway keeping a sharp eye on the hedgerows and watching for snipers or enemy machine gun positions.

The 2d Platoon proceeded toward several small farm buildings. When they came abreast of this hamlet Lomell suddenly jerked Kuhn into a doorway. Alarmed, 1st Sergeant Lomell said to Kuhn, "Didn't you see that Jerry kneeling in the road aiming at us?" Unbelievably, S/Sergeant Kuhn had not, and he was grateful for Lomell's rapid action.

Kuhn glanced outside and saw the enemy soldier still kneeling in the road; the German caught sight of the sergeant and fired twice. A bullet crashed through the door frame just above Kuhn's head. 1st Sergeant Lomell jumped out of a window in order to take the soldier by surprise, but the German ran. Kuhn stepped out to cut him down with his Tommy gun, but the piece would not fire. Upon examination, he found that the clip had been hit. S/Sergeant Kuhn informed Lomell that he was going back to the bluff — only a short distance — in order to retrieve a workable weapon from a dead Ranger.[1]

* * * *

Unit: Company D, 2d Platoon
Location: Black-top highway

Shortly before 8:00 a.m. S/Sergeant Kuhn returned to the squad to find Lomell setting up a roadblock on the coastal highway. 1st Sergeant Lomell had originally counted 22 men in his platoon who had reached the top of the cliff, but due to heavy fighting across the Pointe and along the exit road he lost 10 men in casualties. Nevertheless, Lomell positioned his 12 men on both sides of the black-top road stretched out about 100 yards with an outpost on the far south-west end of his line. This was the first Ranger roadblock established D-Day morning on the main highway.

The D Company men were to cover the west flank toward Grandcamp. Pfc. Len Rubin with his B.A.R. along with T/5 Harley R. Huff, Sgt. Gordon Luning, Pfc. Robert C. Carty, Sgt. Michael Branley, Sgt. Harry Fate, S/Sgt. Larry Johnson and Kuhn settled down in a rain ditch which was covered with high grass.

Within a few minutes, more 2d Platoon Rangers rendezvoused with Lomell: Pvt. Jack Conaboy, T/Sgt. Harvey Koenig, T/5 Henry Stecki and Sgt. Pat McCrone. The men were armed with grenade launchers, small arms weapons, and one bazooka.[2]

1st Sergeant Lomell deployed across from Kuhn and Johnson and covered the same area. The first sergeant kept watch on the exit road and eastward, down the black-top highway. No other Rangers were sighted, but he anticipated seeing Germans at any moment retreating from Omaha Beach.[3]

The Rangers heard movement behind a stone fence. They spied a German looking up and down the highway. Believing the area to be clear, the soldier stepped through the stonewall and ran across the road — right up to the concealed Kuhn. The German had a burp gun slung across his shoulder; he had no idea that he was only inches away from an American bullet. Sergeant Kuhn took a deep breath, jumped up and fired his Tommy gun directly into the man's chest. The soldier ran a few paces and then fell dead.

Johnson whispered to Kuhn, "Hey, Jack, get me his gun." Kuhn leaned out into the road and reached for the gun; he spied another German standing in the opening of the stone fence. The German was aiming right at Sergeant Kuhn. Jack Kuhn knew he was a dead man. "I had no way to protect myself and felt I was about to be shot," he later recalled. But, once again Lomell was watching over the situation. He blasted the German just as he fired at Kuhn. The German bullet barely missed Jack. Lomell had saved Jack's life again.[4]

* * * *

Unit: Company D, 2d Platoon
Location: South of the black-top highway

As D Company established their observation post and roadblock, 1st Sergeant Lomell and S/Sergeant Kuhn noted markings in a sunken road. Lomell recounted the scene.

> . . . It looked like something heavy had been over it [the road] . . . And so Jack and I went down this sunken road not knowing where the hell it was going, but it was going inland and...we came upon this vale, or this little draw with camouflage all over it, and lo and behold, I peeked over this — just pure luck — over this hedgerow and about two hundred yards from the highway I found five 155mm guns in a draw or vale of an orchard . . . all sitting in proper firing condition, the ammunition piled up neatly, everything at the ready, but they were pointed at Utah Beach. They weren't pointed at Omaha Beach.[5]

"Jack, here they are! We've found 'em. Here're the goddamn guns!" Lomell excitedly, but quietly, informed Kuhn. Through the bushes he could see the machines of war, still and serene, but no camouflage could conceal their aspect of death and destruction.

Curiously, Lomell saw no German soldiers directly by the guns. There were piles of ammunition stacked neatly nearby, and the fuses were set on the shells. But where were the artillerymen? Taking another look, they spotted 75 to100 Germans roughly 100 yards away in a corner of a field where it junctured with a sunken farm lane. An officer stood on a vehicle, and the enemy soldiers crowded around him totally unaware of the close proximity of the two Americans (see map 8).

Finding no guards on the guns, Lomell said, "Jack, you cover me; I'm going in there and fix 'em. Keep your eyes on those Krauts." Armed only with his Tommy gun and two thermite grenades, 1st Sergeant Lomell crept over the hedgerow and crawled into the battery. He pulled the pins on two thermite grenades. They opened with an almost imperceptible click. Lomell placed them in the recoils and traversing mechanisms of two of the guns. As the air hit the chemical contents of the grenades, the soldering material trickled out spilling itself into every moving part of the odious machines, fusing and binding the gears in the traversing and elevation mechanisms rendering the guns forever silent. Lomell then smashed the sights on all five guns. Having run out of thermite grenades, the two sergeants hurried as fast as they could back to the roadblock to collect more.[6]

* * * *

Unit: Company E
Location: Southwest of the 155mm guns
As the D Company men carried out their mission, Sgt. Frank A. Rupinski took a patrol from E Company and reconnoitered the area southwest of Company D's roadblock. They were approaching the 155mm battery from the east. Coming in from another direction, and unseen by any D Company men, the E Company squad serendipitously came upon the ammunition dump; the guns were some distance away and were out of sight of Rupinski's patrol. Sergeant Rupinski decided to blow the artillery shells and prepared the charges to do so. After setting the explosives, the E Company men made their get away without being detected by the Germans or D Company.

* * * *

Unit: Company D
Location: Back at the 155mm guns
Lomell and Kuhn, in the meantime, hurried back to the hidden battery in the orchard unaware of Rupinski's team setting up charges that as yet had not gone off. Lomell set out again and repeated the previous procedure in the three remaining 155mm pieces (one of the six guns was never found). The feared and hateful guns would never again belch forth death.

Watching Lomell from the hedgerow, Jack grew nervous. "Hurry up, Len; get out of there," Kuhn quietly warned. 1st Sergeant Lomell had just finished destroying the guns and came up over the hedgerow when,

> . . . the whole place blew up. We thought it was a short round from the *Texas*, because the *Texas* was giving us fire support . . . we went flying and ram rods, rocks, dust and everything came down on us. We got up and ran like scared rabbits as fast as we could to get back to our men at the road block, less than 200 yards away.[7]

The Germans were just as startled as the two Rangers and ran toward the battery. They discovered their big guns and ammo dump were useless, and the culprits had vanished.

* * * *

Unit: Company D, 2d and 1st Platoons
Location: Back at roadblock on black-top highway

It was now about 8:15-8:30 a.m., and with a rush of adrenalin, Lomell and Kuhn returned to their roadblock. They needed to get word back to Rudder about the success of their mission.

Sgts. Harry Fate and Gordon Luning volunteered to take separate routes back to the Pointe. The men would inform the colonel that the 155mm guns were destroyed; all German communications had been cut and destroyed by Sgt. Harvey Koenig, 2d Platoon, D Company, and the Company D roadblock was solidly in place. The two sergeants were also directed to get further orders from Lieutenant Colonel Rudder. [8]

Shortly after Lomell's men left, about eight or nine 1st Platoon, D Company soldiers reached the roadblock. They were happy to hear the good news, but this was no time or place for a celebration.

* * * *

Farm building on exit road about 200 yards from the highway.
Small Unit Action

One of the exit roads halfway between the Pointe and the black-top highway. D Company and E Company encountered scattered opposition from enemy groups along this road. *Small Unit Action.*

The Liberation of Pointe du Hoc

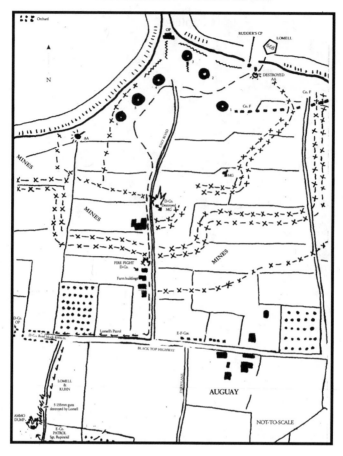

Map 8

June 6, 7:10 a.m.-8:15 a.m. Company D, 2d Platoon, route to the black-top highway. At 8:00 a.m. Lomell set up a roadblock on the black-top highway. Kuhn and Lomell then find and destroy the 155mm guns just south of the main highway. Sergeant Rupinski, E Company, and his patrol approach the battery from the east and blow the German ammunition dump.

Notes to Chapter 11

[1] Astor, 174-175, and Lomell's notes to the author July 29, 1999.

[2] George Kerchner recalled that he reached D Company roadblock sometime around 8:00 a.m. (phone conversation August 14, 1999). Len Lomell and other 2d Platoon soldiers do not remember seeing Kerchner at this time (phone conversation August 14, 1999 and interview August 21, 1999), and stated that in their recollection Kerchner arrived out at the roadblock sometime after 9:00 a.m.

[3] Phone conversation with Len Lomell, July 22, 1999. See also Lane, 129 and Astor, 175.

[4] Astor, 175.

[5] Lomell, 12-13. See also Astor, 175.

[6] Notes to author by Len Lomell, July 29, 1999. A thermite grenade contains highly volatile incendiary material. When the pin is pulled and the air hits it, it turns into molten-like fluid that welds moving parts and gears together rendering them inoperable (notes to author by Len Lomell, August 13, 1999).

[7] Lomell 14-15. Notes to author by Lomell, August 13, 1999. See also Lane, 130. Lomell and Kuhn at the time did not know who blew up the ammunition dump. They found out years later at a reunion that it was Rupinski's Company E patrol.

[8] Lomell, 14-15. Kerchner does not remember Luning going back to the command post (phone call to Kerchner August 17, 1999). But Len Lomell of 2d Platoon, Luning's unit, does recall that Sergeant Luning was one of the messengers.

Chapter 12

"Praise the Lord":
9:00 a.m.-11:00 a.m.

Unit: Headquarters Company
Location: Near the Pointe, command post

The main objectives, destroying the 155mm guns, establishing roadblocks and cutting the German communications were accomplished by 8:30 a.m. Sgt. Gordon Luning and Sgt. Harry Fate, from 2d Platoon, D Company, arrived at the command post just before 9:00 a.m. Luning told Lieutenant Eikner the great news, but Rudder was not with the lieutenant when the message came in. Upon finding the colonel, Eikner passed the word that the big guns were destroyed. "Should I send a message?" the lieutenant asked Rudder. "Yes," Lieutenant Colonel Rudder replied. Lieutenant Eikner used the signal lamp and flickered the appropriate code: *Praise the Lord.* This revealed that the Rangers had reached the top of the cliff and had destroyed the guns.[1] Eikner then prepared one of the carrier pigeons to deliver the message. He slipped a note in a small tube, tied it to the bird and released it. The pigeon flew in circles over the command post and landed right in front of Headquarters. Lieutenant Eikner threw pebbles at the bird and finally the messenger took off out to sea.[2]

After seeing the pigeon off, the lieutenant relayed the message, "— need ammunition and reinforcements — many casualties."[3] Eikner did not receive an immediate answer, but an hour later the *Satterlee* returned a brief message from Gen. Clarence Huebner, "No reinforcements available — all Rangers have landed [at Omaha]."[4] The men would have to hold the Pointe alone. Although the big guns were demolished and German communications had been cut, the battle for the Pointe was far from over; now the second phase of the mission took shape.

* * * *

Unit: Company D
Location: Going inland

With two thirds of their mission accomplished, Lieutenant Colonel Rudder directed Luning to carry the word back to the road: they were to "hold 'til duly relieved." After a brief rest, Sergeant Luning took off again for Lomell's roadblock.

On his way back Luning bumped into Lieutenant Kerchner; the two men teamed up. As they neared the 40mm anti-aircraft gun position on the far west flank, they decided to once again try to knock it out. The two men hunched down and inched toward the gun. Several Germans, however, had spotted the Rangers and began stalking them. They went unnoticed by the Americans who were focused on the 40mm weapon.

Lieutenant Kerchner took a good look at the gun emplacement, aimed, squeezed the trigger and nothing. Dirt, mud and clay completely clogged the piece. Frustrated, he was forced to field strip his weapon and clean it. The lieutenant quickly reassembled his gun, but at that point the Germans behind them began firing. Luning and Kerchner realized they were the ones being hunted and called off their assault. They both advanced toward D Company's roadblock as fast as they could go.[5]

The Liberation of Pointe du Hoc

* * * *

Unit: Company F
Location: Near the cliff and German anti-aircraft gun
While Kerchner and Luning battled the dangerous west-flank gun, Capt. Otto Masny, F Company, established a defensive perimeter on the left flank of the battalion's command post. Bullets from the German anti-aircraft gun zipped dangerously close to Masny. Fuming, the big captain grabbed the nearest available soldiers to take a turn at silencing the menacing piece.

A 60mm mortar section from Company E joined Masny's make-shift unit. Besides the mortar, Masny's team was armed with a 30-caliber machine gun. The men headed down the left exit road and moved about 100 yards south of gun position No. 6. Near the casemate Masny turned west and continued down a small farm lane which led directly to the rear of the anti-aircraft position.

Advancing another 100 yards on the farm lane, the Rangers scattered. The entire area lit up; German riflemen blazed away, machine gunners sprayed the road; mortar and artillery fire rained down on Masny's squad. Then the anti-aircraft gun opened up. Masny's men hid in the craters and attempted to return fire. Every deadly projectile which could take human life and maim and disfigure was showered upon them. All commands were drowned in this terrible storm but once again their training showed. The American mortar crew set up and began pummeling the German sector.

Abruptly, the Germans near the anti-aircraft weapon waved a white flag; the firing subsided. Two Rangers stood up to accept German prisoners; Masny, however, was not fully convinced of the enemy's intentions. The hair stood up on the back of his neck as he shouted to his men, "Stay down! You guys get down!" But the warning came too late. At the same time, a German machine-gunner opened on the exposed Rangers; with terrible effect, the blasts literally ripped the men apart. The battle resumed.[6]

* * * *

Unit: Headquarters Company
Location: Command Post, farm ruins inland, Masny's position, and back to Headquarters
Rudder heard the pandemonium off to the west where Masny's men were pinned down. His head filled with unanswered questions: What was happening on the Pointe? Were his Rangers giving or taking the beating? Where were the German snipers deployed? None of the other squads, except for D Company's Sergeants Luning and Fate, had reported to Headquarters. Rudder grew anxious. He glanced around and yelled to a private standing nearby, "Fruhling, is your radio working?"

"Yes, sir!" Pfc. Robert A. Fruhling of D Company replied. Fruhling carried the only working SCR 300, and the radio was tuned to Lieutenant Eikner's frequency. Rudder and Fruhling set out to try and kill a sniper harassing the command post and to make contact with some of the squads. As they cautiously proceeded toward one of the exit roads, a machine-gunner from Company E joined the colonel and private.

The three men reached some bombed out farm buildings. This was the same area where D Company, 2d Platoon, had earlier knocked out a machine gun nest which had tried to deny them access to the exit road. German troops had reoccupied the ruins. They opened up on Rudder's detachment. The American machine-gunner answered with short bursts. Fruhling radioed a message to Eikner at the command post.

Battle debris on one of the many farm lanes used by the Rangers.
Lisko's Ranger Box, USAMHI.

Bombed out farm buildings along one of the exit roads.
Photo taken by G.K. Hodenfield. Lisko's Ranger Box, USAMHI.

Lieutenant Eikner heard the urgent message on his radio. His commander needed naval support. Using the signal lamp, Eikner once again contacted a ship. Her huge guns belched forth. In just a few minutes the Germans were gone. Rudder's reconnaissance, however, was cut short when he was wounded again. Fruhling and the machine-gunner covered Lieutenant Colonel Rudder as the three headed back for the command post.

* * * *

Unit: Company F
Location: Near the German anti-aircraft gun, west flank

Masny's men were still stranded near gun position 6; fire from the anti-aircraft gun was venomous and produced heavy casualties. A piece of shrapnel sliced into Captain Masny's arm. German artillery fell all around them; every shot seemed to tell. It was time to clear out. "Every man for himself!"

Each Ranger retraced his steps. Four were killed, and most of the men were wounded. They inched their way down the farm lane to the exit road. Two more Rangers fell, shot dead by a sniper's bullets. The mortar men abandoned their weapon; they had expended their ammunition in any case and were now seeking only to survive. Everything was in shambles.

Captain Masny waited for his men to leave and brought up the rear. As the captain retreated he bumped into Pfc. Fruhling and the machine-gunner. The three men stayed together. Under devastating German fire, Masny suggested they make a run for a nearby shell crater. They took off running; a sniper drew a bead on them and raked the area.

Hit twice, Masny fell into a crater headfirst. Pfc. Fruhling moved with difficulty, the cumbersome radio strapped to his back. A bullet struck Fruhling's helmet; he crashed hard into the crater. Blood ran down his face; his vision was blurred and his head rang. Miraculously, the bullet penetrated his helmet but bounced off his skull. Captain Masny looked at Fruhling. They had become separated from the machine-gunner and had only two rounds left in Pfc. Fruhling's pistol. The German sniper sat in a tree out of pistol range.

Masny ordered Fruhling to take off his radio and destroy it. The private plugged his last two bullets into the radio, and the two Rangers zig-zagged as quickly as possible toward Headquarters. Trying not to attract attention, they moved from crater to carter. In one hole they stumbled upon S/Sgt. James E. Fulton, F Company.

Sergeant Fulton lay with his legs crossed, hands behind his head and his B.A.R. across his chest with bandoliers of bullets around his neck. Thinking the sergeant might be injured, Masny inquired, "Are you hit?" The sergeant emphatically replied, "Hell, no, Cap'n. Ah'm just restin'. This is the third load of ammo I've hauled around this mornin' and I'm tared." Masny, hopping mad, yelled, "Well, get that damn B.A.R. workin' and get that Kraut sniper that's chasin' us, will ya?"

"Sure, Sir, jist point me at 'im," Sergeant Fulton nonchalantly responded. Fulton slowly laid his B.A.R. at the edge of the shell crater; Masny and Fruhling peeked over the lip. The German sniper had climbed down from the tree and was advancing on his wounded prey. Captain Masny placed his helmet on his Tommy gun and raised it tentatively above the lip of the crater.

Seeing the American helmet, the sniper stopped and aimed his rifle. Fulton emptied his B.A.R. clip at the German — 20 rounds; the man was dead before he hit the ground. Relieved that their stalker had been killed, Masny and Fruhling dragged themselves to the medical station near the command post. They were hurt, but they were alive![7]

Several failed assaults on the west flank anti-aircraft gun cost the 2d Ranger Battalion between 15-20 men. Several attempts to blow the anti-aircraft gun were made by the ships, but the position was too far inland, out of range even for the big Naval guns.[8]* The position was either surrendered or finally knocked out by the Rangers on D+1.[9]

Meanwhile, Rudder makes his way down the exit road and is stopped by machine gun fire; but Allied Naval ships take out the machine gun position and the colonel returns to his CP.

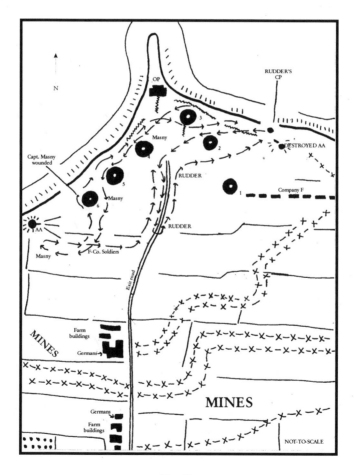

Map 9
The elusive Anti-Aircraft gun position. Captain Masny and his patrol make their way toward the anti-aircraft gun but are turned back.

Notes to Chapter 12

[1] Ambrose 410 and 412. See also Eikner, 12.

[2] Telephone conversation with James Eikner, July 25, 1999. Eikner never found out what happened to the bird.

[3] *Omaha Beachhead,* 91.

[4] *Ibid.*

[5] Kerchner, 24-25. Kerchner's diary and oral history seem to differ on this episode. In his diary he implies that he was at Lomell's roadblock much earlier than 2d Platoon personnel remember, and that he and Luning tried to go back to Rudder's command post but were cut off by four "Jerries." Kerchner and Luning eluded the enemy and returned to the roadblock, see Kerchner's diary, pg. 6.

[6] Lane, 134-135.

[7] The episode concerning Masny and Fruhling can be found in Lane, 136-138.

[8] *Ibid.,* 139.

[9] Interview with Len Lomell, August 21, 1999.

Chapter 13

"I Think You Got the Bastard":
Counterattacks

Unit: Company F
Location: Left flank near the cliff

At the beginning of the battle the Germans did not attempt any serious counterattacks. For the most part, small pockets of enemy soldiers held their positions near the cliff and laid down harassing fire. As snipers hunted down the Rangers, however, a larger German contingency was organizing farther inland. The worst was yet to come.

* * * *

Unit: Company D
Location: Inland at the roadblock on the black-top highway, west of the exit road

Just prior to the first German counterattack, about mid-morning, Lieutenant Kerchner and Luning returned to D Company's roadblock. Sergeant Luning relayed the commander's message: they were to hold their roadblock position to the last man or until duly relieved. Lieutenant Kerchner glanced around and counted how many of his men had made it: Lomell, Kuhn, Sgt. Lawrence Johnson, Koenig, Sgt. Lester Arthur, Sgt. Emory Jones, Branley, McLaughlin, Flanagan, Sweany, T/5 Henry Stecki, Luning, Huff, Pfc. Iriving Hoover, Pfc. Robert Carty, Fate, Rubin, Sgt. Robert Austin and Pfc. James Blum. Including himself, the lieutenant counted twenty.[1]

The small band maintained their roadblock and continued to keep a close eye out on the black-top road and the fields around them. 1st Sergeant Lomell peeked over a five-foot stonewall bordering the black-top road. Lomell sighted about 50 Germans forming up farther down the main highway heading west and advancing from the direction of Omaha Beach. Unaware of the Rangers' location, the enemy deployed in a disciplined manner. German scouts led the way.

* * * *

Unit: Company F
Location: Left flank near the cliff

Lomell may have spotted part of the first major counter offensive. At approximately 11:00 a.m., in Lieutenant Wintz's F Company sector on the left flank, the Germans launched their first organized assault. Wintz deployed his men just east of the base of the Pointe.

Coming from the direction of St. Pierre-du-Mont (south-east), F Company observed German helmets off in the distance. Setting up a machine gun, the assailants opened up on F Company. Their assault was supported by artillery and mortar fire. The Rangers remained calm, hunkered down, and fired their rifles. Fortunately for Wintz's platoon, the artillery and mortar shells landed away from their position.

One of F Company's own mortar crew, commanded by S/Sgt. Eugene E. Elder, saw and heard the assault. Elder recalled the tense moments:

> ... Sergeant Merle Stinnette told me there was a counterattack coming in on our left. We swung the mortars around, and I gave a compass reading and yardage to the gun crew. The Germans were coming in close, and we didn't have much time for any other preparations and the range card wouldn't accommodate this small, short, range. We ended up firing 35 yards from our own position, much closer than it is standard, but we broke up the counterattack.[2]

Even though Elder's team ran low on ammo they were able to help knock back the Germans.

Wintz's riflemen continued to put up a resistance as well. The assault lasted for about an hour. By then the Germans had had enough, and they could be seen gradually withdrawing.[3]

* * * *

Unit: Headquarters Comapny
Location: Command Post

With Elder's mortar crew running short of ammunition, Corporal Lisko and a comrade stationed in the command post were directed to carry some to the F Company mortar men deployed about ten or twelve craters away.

The two Headquarters Rangers grabbed a handful of mortar shells and their carbines and headed toward Company F's mortar crew. Lisko described the scene:

> ... 4 or 5 bomb craters away a German saw us and jumped up very quickly; he fired at my ranger friend. All the bullets hit the side of the crater. The German must have been pretty nervous; he just got up, fired and ducked back down. A man gets very frightened when things like this happen, so much so that the ranger in front of me could not control his bodily functions -

> I was lying on my back waiting for the German to fire at us again, but nothing happened. I guess he was as scared as we were, and he must have crawled back to another position. While I was waiting, my ranger friend pulled off his pants and cleaned himself as best as he could with his underwear ... That's the kind of thing that happens in combat. Most soldiers do not tell other people about it; they talk about it among themselves ... .[4]

Hearing no Germans in the other crater, Lisko and his companion delivered the mortars to Company F's mortar team; the two men safely returned to the command post. Upon their return Lisko and his buddy learned that the guns had been destroyed.

* * * *

Unit: Headquarters Company
Location: Command Post

Activity around the command post continued after Corporal Lisko returned. Wounded Rangers straggled in; messengers from units stationed out and near the black-top highway hurried in and out with reports and orders, and prisoners were dropped off to be guarded by the men of Headquarters.

About mid-afternoon, the Rangers at the command post discovered a bunker directly in front of their position. Two doors, however, had been blocked by debris. Rudder directed Lisko and Cpl. Steve Liscinsky to take two prisoners and have them walk toward the bunker and get the door unblocked, and then have the German prisoners open the doors.

Lisko and Liscinsky pointed their carbines at two captives.

> [One was a] . . . young blonde German . . . we asked them to climb the crater to open the door. The young man was the first to start climbing; when he got to the top, he stood straight up and bullets hit him directly in the chest. He fell face down with his hands still clasped over his head. After seeing this, the other prisoner, who was older, turned around quickly, fell on his back and put his hands in a praying motion, begging us not to send him up. He must have thought we were sending him up to see if anyone would fire at him, so Col. Rudder said to forget about it. Then, we went back to our radio.

Half an hour later, I crawled up along the edge and saw the dead German. He was lying there, face down with blood coming out of his back.[5]

The dead German prisoner was a grim reminder that the enemy was all over the Pointe, hiding in tunnels and underground bunkers. It was an inexpressibly somber and depressing realization. Turning their attention away from the bunker, Lisko accompanied several wounded Rangers down to the beach.

* * * *

Units: Company D and squads from Companies E and F
Location: About one mile inland

While Headquarters men aided the injured men, the Ranger contingency continued to grow along the main highway throughout the day. By 4:00 p.m. about 60 soldiers from all three companies had rendezvoused. In addition to the Rangers, three 101st Airborne paratroopers had joined with the battalion. They had jumped in the early morning hours of D-Day and had been scheduled to land 15 miles away, north of Carentan. Scattered to the winds, most of the Airborne fell far from their drop zone. Under the circumstances, both parties were glad to make contact with one another.

With more Rangers gathering, their battle line extended about a mile long. On the left flank (east) Company F deployed near the village of AuGuay; Company E assembled to their right, and on the far right flank (west) D Company still manned its roadblock. They expected Germans to advance from the Grandcamp area.

* * * *

Unit: Company F
Locations: South of the black-top highway

Earlier in the day Sgts. Bill Petty and William M. McHugh of F Company had advanced to a position south of the highway, re-deploying near a creek and setting up a forward observation post. Around noon Petty headed back to the line near the black-top road in order to acquire another rifle for one of his men. As Petty entered the area, Sgt. James R. Alexander blasted his B.A.R. in the direction of the main road where two Germans had appeared. One enemy fell. Sergeant Petty said excitedly to Alexander, "I think you got the bastard; let's check him out." The Americans carried their B.A.R.s at their hips, ready to fire. Three other Rangers joined the two sergeants. Alexander walked to the body to examine it; Petty nonchalantly sat on a wooden fence and stared at the dead soldier. Suddenly voices from a nearby ditch startled the Rangers. Sergeant Petty quickly jumped down. Three Germans rose up out of the ditch yelling, "*Kamerad*! *Kamerad*!" Their hands were raised high. Sgt. Walter J. Borowski sprayed bullets into the hedgerow. Two more Germans swiftly jumped up with arms raised.

The Rangers walked their prizes to Companies E and F command post where they located a lieutenant and a non-commissioned officer. Approximately forty Germans were captured on D-Day and held in a field just south of the black-top highway and east of the exit road. After dropping the Germans off, Petty and nine more Rangers walked back to the advance outpost at the creek. A small bridge and a farm lane lay about 150 yards to the west of Petty's position. Throughout the day small groups of Germans were viewed crossing this bridge and heading toward Grandcamp. When an enemy group strayed within range of Petty and his B.A.R. he opened fire.[6]

* * * *

Unit: Company F
Location: Left flank inland, west end of Wintz's line

Near the Pointe fellow F Company Rangers in Wintz's platoon had been resting after they repulsed the first counterattack. But around 4:00 p.m. all hell broke loose. This time the second assault focused on the western end of Wintz's line. It was the same area where Jack Richards had been killed. T/5 Herm Stein had remained there after convincing Pfc. Cloise Manning to act as assistant to the B.A.R. Just as they got squared away, the Germans launched their second attack, zeroing in on their line. Artillery and mortars fell all around Stein and Manning.

The Americans made a mad dash. With most of the shells landing to their left, they automatically drifted to the right. They continued to move through about five or six shell craters and were almost in line with Rudder's command post. The German artillery stopped.

Seconds later Stein and Manning heard small arms fire. The two Rangers could not tell at what they were shooting. Herm Stein explained the situation:

> . . . Darned if we could figure it out. The firing came ever closer. We finally realized they were firing on the dormant C.P. Their present path would bring them very close to our flank. There were two squads of six or seven men each, one had a machine gun. We decided to blast the automatic weapon when it got opposite us. Away went the B.A.R., along with Cloise firing his M-1. The bullets found their mark for our blasts had quieted the action. We still had the other squad to contend with so I loaded a grenade and a grenade launcher on to Cloise's rifle. He fired and nothing, Cripe's! I forgot to pull the pin. We got another off that fell short.[7]

Stein's and Manning's quick response disorganized the German assault. But unlike the previous counterattack, the enemy reorganized and rallied. The second wave extended beyond F Company's flank.

Sgt. Murrell F. Stinnette, in another crater, yelled to Stein, "What's all the noise?" "We've pinned down a couple of German squads out there," T/5 Stein replied. "Give me the range," Stinnette directed Stein. Stein didn't think a mortar could be geared at such a close proximity, but the "sinewy tough ex-merchant mariner quickly estimated his distance to the Section Leader, Elder, the master of short range work."[8]

Sergeant Elder's first mortar round fell among the advancing Germans. They swiftly retreated; Elder then turned his mortar south and sent shells right into the craters. The explosions flushed the enemy out of hiding, and Stein blasted the withdrawing Germans with his B.A.R. The extra muscle that Elder applied brought gleeful relief to Cloise Manning and Herm Stein. Sergeant Elder expended 75 rounds during the afternoon assaults. Eight other riflemen from F Company also came to aid Stein and Manning. With their combined efforts, the Rangers beat back the second counterattack.

* * * *

Unit: Company F
Location: Between the black-top road and Rudder's command post

While the second German attack was occurring near the Pointe, Lt. Jacob Hill, out on the black-top highway, was asked to return to Lieutenant Colonel Rudder's command post and report F Company's situation on the main road. Pfc. John Bacho joined the lieutenant on this dangerous assignment.

As they cautiously headed back to the bluff the two Rangers heard machine gun fire just east of the exit road. Hill, eager to take out another death-dealing enemy position, crept toward the sound of the weapon; Bacho followed. It was only two fields away from the exit road. Hill and Bacho hid behind a hedgerow and carefully peeked over the brush. About 12 Germans were relaxing and talking.

Hill could have quietly exited the area, leaving the enemy soldiers behind, but he was here to do a job. The two men retrieved grenades from their ammunition belts, pulled their pins, and simultaneously threw them over the hedgerow. To their dismay neither grenade exploded but landed harmlessly in the midst of their opponents.

Furious, the Germans hurled their potato-mashers over the hedgerow toward the two G.Is; a grenade burst right between Hill and Bacho. At the same time one of the antagonists crashed through the hedgerow firing his pistol-machine gun. Bullets shredded Lieutenant Hill's chest, and he fell dead. Bacho remained unharmed. His lieutenant was down and Bacho's fighting blood was up; he was insensible to danger. He threw his remaining grenades at the Germans as fast as he could pull the pins. One of his bombs exploded spewing out burning white phosphorous. Seconds later a bullet passed through Bacho's helmet; he toppled to the ground but was unhurt. Realizing he was outnumbered, the private lay still trying to appear to be dead.

The squad of Germans approached the Rangers. They saw the private's hollow helmet lying close by with a neat hole through it. Lieutenant Hill lay with his chest grotesquely opened and his life's blood soaking the Normandy soil. The Germans moved on. Bacho remained there until nightfall. He then made his way back to Rudder's command post.[9]

* * * *

Units: Make-shift unit from Companies D, E, and F
Location: Cliff perimeter
When the sound of Hill's skirmish dwindled, and the Germans from the second attack withdrew, an uneasy, peculiar calmness fell on the Pointe. The remaining daylight hours passed uneventfully, and, in the late afternoon, Captain Masny gathered men from all three companies, including some of the walking-wounded, and established a perimeter to the front and left (east) side of the command post.

* * * *

Unit: Company D
Location: Roadblock to the right of Cos. E and F
At the inland Ranger positions the men had heard the intense fire fight near the Pointe and became more alert when they noted the noise subsiding. The Germans might be re-organizing in another part of the Pointe, or they might retreat right into the backs of he Rangers on the black-top highway.

Sure enough, minutes later, D Company men spotted the Germans from the second counterattack withdrawing (see map 10). Lieutenant Kerchner recalled the tense scene:

> . . . a large group of Germans moved down the road behind the hedgerow right opposite where we were. We were in this ditch along one side of this very narrow road and directly across the road, not 25 feet away, was this hedgerow and walking right along behind this hedgerow were 50 or 60 Germans. We decided that it wasn't a smart thing to start firing at them because we could only see their helmets and heads, and if we would have fired and

disclosed our position, since we were in a ditch, we would have been sitting ducks for them; they could have thrown grenades over. We didn't fire at this stage, but we noticed that these Germans moved down around our flank and started heading inland..[at the next farm road going in that direction].[10]

The enemy was withdrawing, but Company D personnel realized they were still greatly outnumbered. As their training had taught them, they held their fire and remained hidden and silent as the enemy passed within inches of them. They would wait to strike at a more favorable time.

* * * *

Though the Rangers occupied the Pointe, and had thwarted two major assaults, Pointe-du-Hoc had not been liberated as of the evening of June 6. Communications between Rudder's CP and the men deployed inland remained difficult to achieve. The Germans continued to occupy many areas in no man's land. "It was a new kind of warfare, a crazy kind. The Jerries knew every inch of the terrain; they had the place taped right down to the last little shell hole. They had long, deep tunnels through which they would dash, firing first from one spot and then another," Lieutenant Hodenfield stated.[11]

The Rangers in their trenches kept a diligent lookout for enemy movement.

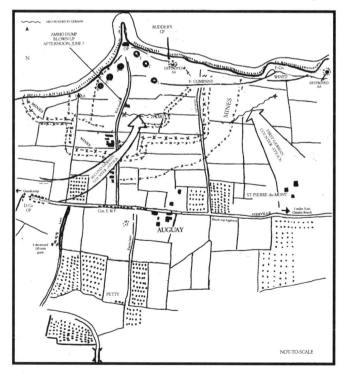

Map 10
June 6, 11:00 a.m. and 4:00 p.m.

Morning and afternoon attacks on the Pointe repulsed by F Company, elements of E Company and HQ Company. Also, disposition of Companies E, F and D about one mile inland during the morning and afternoon.

Notes to Chapter 13

[1] Kerchner's diary, 5.
[2] Elder, Eisenhower Center, 4. Elder puts the counterattack around 10:00 a.m. or 11:00 a.m.
[3] Lisko, 140.
[4] *Ibid.,* 141.
[5] *Ibid.*, 141-142.
[6] Story of Petty can be found in Lane, 144-145.
[7] Herm Stein.
[8] *Ibid.*
[9] Lane, 142-143.
[10] Kerchner, 25. Also, Len Lomell's notes to the author, August 13, 1999.
[11] Chapelie, Hodenfield's testimony, 164.

Chapter 14

"Hold 'til Duly Relieved":
First Night Attack

Unit: Headquarters Company
Location: Down on the beach

Casualties had mounted as the day wore on. The wounded gathered at the command post and down on the beach. Inland and on the bluff the German artillery and mortar fire continued to inflict numerous injuries among the Rangers. Below the cliff, however, the American wounded were fairly well protected as most of the shells flew harmlessly over their location and into the water.

Corporal Lisko, HQ Company, and the Ranger medics tended to the injured. At the top of the precipice the medics strapped wounded G.I.s onto stretchers and carefully lowered them down to Lisko. Once on the beach, two or three German prisoners carefully lifted the wounded soldiers onto another stretcher and carried them to a small cave.

One American suffered a huge gash between his hip and his knee; the fatty tissue was out, and his leg was open. When the prisoners reached to pick the man up, one of the Germans grabbed the man's mangled leg. The Ranger let out a blood curdling scream. Lisko whipped around and hit the captive in the face with the back of his hand; the German fell to the ground. As he got back up, Corporal Lisko angrily demanded that he be more careful.

Lisko completed the task of overseeing the placement of the wounded in the relative safety of the cave. He then turned his attention to two sailors on the beach. These sailors had been stranded on the Pointe when their boat sank. They helped guard the prisoners who were tending the American wounded.

As new prisoners arrived the two sailors demanded that they hand over their wrist watches and other valuables. When asked to remove his watch, one German refused. One can assume that a loved one had given the item to the man, and he did not wish to relinquish the memento. The sailor grabbed the end of his rifle and jabbed the prisoner in the stomach; reluctantly, the German handed the man his watch.

"Why are you doing that?" Lisko angrily inquired of the sailor.

The man replied curtly, "Hey! Ranger — we're collecting these things; we're taking them back to the boat, and we're going to get a lot of money for them as souvenirs."

Corporal Lisko reminded the sailor of the current situation on the Pointe. "Sailor, you may not even get back to the boat. We are surrounded by Germans on three sides. We may all be captured, and if you are captured and they find all the things you've taken from the German prisoners, you're a dead man. They'll almost surely believe that you killed the prisoners to get the souvenirs." The sailors did not seem to worry. Lisko had said all that he could, and he headed back up to the command post.[1]

* * * *

Unit: Headquarters

The Liberation of Pointe du Hoc

Location: Command Post

When Corporal Lisko returned to Headquarters twilight was approaching. He counted at least 20 Rangers wounded or dying. Trying to disregard the suffering of his comrades, Lisko ate a hasty meal of bitter chocolate, tasteless cakes —"dog biscuits," and a cup of soup. Ignoring the agony of his friends, however, did not work. Whenever Corporal Lisko looked up from his meal he saw the pain in the men's eyes.

"Can I give the wounded a couple of spoonfuls of soup?" The corporal asked Doc Block. The doctor quickly responded, "Oh, yes it would be helpful."

Lisko moved from one man to another. "Open your mouth," he would plead with them. Many of the Rangers were too weak and could hardly do so, but they did not moan or complain.

Corporal Lisko clearly remembered seeing Capt. Jonathan Harwood. Captain Harwood was the Army Shore Fire Control officer who had been mortally wounded by friendly fire. He was lying on a stretcher, covered by a blanket. Lisko saw that the soldier was not moving and was only barely breathing, nevertheless he inquired about giving the man some soup. Dr. Block, fighting back tears, stated, "No, he is not going to need it; he'll be dead in a couple of hours." Harwood and Block were both from Chicago and had known one another before the war. The doctor could do very little for his friend or for the other dying Rangers.[2]

Caring for the wounded out in the open was not practicable so Block, his medics and several other HQ Company Rangers moved the wounded into a concrete bunker. Hodenfield described the crude hospital.

> . . . [it was a] subterranean chamber near by with sixteen bunks, and here [Block] established a sort of base hospital where he worked all night with a flickering candle and sometimes a flashlight. At times there were so many patients that men had to lie in the command post until, maybe, one of the other patients would die or could be patched up well enough to go back out — maybe to fight . . . .[3]

Once the wounded were safely in the bunker, the Headquarters Rangers, Lieutenant Colonel Rudder and Lieutenant Colonel Trevor (the British officer who had been wounded) sat in the command post sipping coffee. Trevor lit his pipe. Rudder looked at Trevor and asked, "What do you think will happen next?" Within ear-shot of the young Rangers the British officer replied, "Never have I been so convinced of anything in my life as that I will either be a prisoner of war or a casualty by morning."[4]

The effect of his statement was immediate. A kind of shiver ran through the huddled mass on the brow of the cliff. A melancholy feeling fell upon Lisko and the other HQ Rangers. The corporal imagined the Germans storming the command post and shooting them all down like dogs. Lisko then looked up and saw Lieutenant Colonel Rudder standing in the HQ; he did not display any outward anxiety, though he was deep in thought about the inevitable night-time counterattacks. Corporal Lisko, however, could not read his commander's mind. He saw only the calm control and stern resolve of his colonel. The young corporal knew that Rudder had led them through the morning and afternoon battles and that somehow he would see them through the night.

Concrete bunker where Doc Block set up his aid station, on the cliff.

Rangers at the command post take a rare break, June 6, '44.
Left: Cpl. Lou Lisko, Center: Cpl. Steve Liscinsky, Right: Lt. Elmer Vermeer
Taken by Lieutenant Hodenfield. Lisko Ranger Box, USAMHI

The Liberation of Pointe du Hoc

Rangers at Headquarters.
Lieutenant Colonel Trevor, British commando, at lower right hand corner with bandaged head.
Lieutenant Eikner is near the center of the photo drinking from his canteen. Taken by Lieutenant
Hodenfield. Lisko Ranger Box, USAMHI

While Lieutenant Colonel Rudder looked calm to young Corporal Lisko, the colonel was actually quite concerned over his battalion's situation. He still did not know if the Invasion had succeeded. Where were his reinforcements? Ammunition was running low, and there was little drinking water. A large group of Germans had advanced from Isigny and assembled south of the highway. It seemed they had plenty of weapons, ammunition, and an unlimited amount of reinforcements. To make matters worse the 40mm anti-aircraft gun to the west was still operational.

In addition, the Germans controlled the area between Rudder's cliff perimeter and the black-top road position. Little communication was getting through to either parties, but they all knew that the enemy would strike sometime in the night. With no reinforcements in sight from the other Ranger units and the 29th Division at Omaha Beach, the situation seemed grim. One of the only things in Rudder's favor was that the Germans did not know how many Americans were on the Pointe. They would be cautious; and do everything in their power to make the enemy think there were many more Rangers on the Pointe than there truly were. Two battle fronts had formed — one near the bluff and one farther inland.

* * * *

Units: D Company, E Company and F Company
Location: Inland south of the black-top highway

Although it was late in the evening it was still light in the French countryside. In order to have more daylight in which to fight, the Allies operated on double day light savings time, pushing the time back two hours.

Several brave volunteers had traversed through no-man's land to carry messages back and forth between Rudder's command post and the battle line on the black-top highway. It was a precarious journey. When they spotted a courier, the Germans would pop up from their underground hideaways, shoot, and disappear only to reappear about 50 to 75 yards away and take more pot shots at the runner.

A few messages had already gotten through. Earlier, when Luning and Fate had returned from the Pointe, they had delivered one of the last messages from Rudder which directed the men of D, E, and F Companies, approximately 60 soldiers, "to hold till duly relieved," and to set up a night-time defensive perimeter.[5]

Kerchner informed Lieutenant Arman, Company F, and Lieutenant Lapres, Company E, of Rudder's directive. The lieutenant also told them about seeing a large number of Germans massed to the southwest. As ranking officer at the black-top position, Lieutenant Arman discussed the present situation with Lapres and Kerchner. They all agreed the enemy would attempt to break their line as soon as it got dark. The officers concluded that they needed to reconfigure the line of defense.

East of the junction of the exit road and the black-top road, narrow fields bordered the south side of the highway. Traveling south, hedgerows, running east-west, acted as a natural boundary for the fields. The hedgerow position provided a good post for the 40 Company E and F Rangers.

* * * *

Unit: Company F
Location: South of the black-top highway
Looking over the hedgerows, the Rangers saw orchards sloping down to a creek. On the other side of the creek lay a small valley. Germans had dug trenches and foxholes on the northern side of the hedgerows. F Company deployed 200 yards east of a small farm lane — which ran north-south — along the trench line. Sergeant Petty, Company F, with 7 other soldiers maintained their advance position near the creek (see map 11).[6]

* * * *

Unit: Company E
Location: South of the black-top highway
E Company occupied about 200 yards of the hedgerow west of the lane.[7] The officers from Companies E and F set up a command post at a dugout near the farm lane (see map 11). S/Sgt. Robert A. Honhart and T/5 Leroy S. Thompson, Company E, nestled down about 75 yards south of E Company's main line, and Sgt. Hayward A. Robey, Company E, carrying a B.A.R., set up just south of Arman's and Leagans' command post.

* * * *

Lane leading south from black-top highway, along east side of fields held by advance group of Rangers during D-Day. Arman and Lapres command post was about 300 yards down this trail.
Small Unit Action

Unit: Company D
Location: South of the black-top highway, right flank of inland position

In order to bolster their right flank, Lieutenant Kerchner moved his company off he black-top road and advanced a short distance south to connect with E and F Companies. Kerchner then deployed his unit in a right angle. Twenty D Company Rangers (12 from 2d Platoon and 8 from 1st Platoon) faced west behind a hedgerow; 1st Sergeant Lomell set up in the center of this line. Lieutenant Kerchner and Pfc. Leonard Rubin, armed with a B.A.R., established a command post in a corner of this hedgerow where D Company's left flank joined with Company E's right flank. Kerchner sent Sgt. Michael J. Branley and Pfc. Robert C. Carty out about 50 yards west of their position. 1st Sergeant Lomell directed three men from 2d Platoon, one armed with a B.A.R., to set up a listening post 100 yards in the north-west corner of the field where the lane intersected with the highway — the same area where D Company's roadblock had been stationed.[8]

* * * *

Unit: Company A, 1st Platoon, 5th Rangers
Location: South of the black-top highway, near Arman's command post

Around 6:00 p.m. or 7:00 p.m. an advanced group of about 23 Rangers from Company A, 1st Platoon, 5th Rangers broke through the German line. When they passed the small village of AuGuay they met advanced units from Companies F and E, 2d Ranger. Lt. Charles H. Parker, Jr., led the 5th Ranger contingent. They had fought their way from Omaha Beach. The 5th Rangers were immediately interspersed throughout the 2d Battalion's left flank. A few even joined Petty's squad.

Lieutenants Kerchner, Arman, and Leagans were glad to see the reinforcements even though there were so few. Kerchner recalled:

> . . . We were so happy to see him [Parker]; these were the first men from Omaha that we saw, the first time we realized that the invasion was there to stay. There were other men down there, and eventually they were going to come up and join us.[9]

Though the additional men strengthened their inland battle position, the Rangers still only numbered about 85 men and were sorely outnumbered. In addition, the 2d Ranger officers were concerned about a shortage of ammunition. The B.A.R. men were especially low in ammo. To make matters worse, U.S. grenades were scarce. German grenades, "potato mashers," however, were found in plenty. In addition to the lack of ammo, some men had lost or broken their weapons. The Rangers picked up enemy rifles and collected as much ammunition from the dead as possible. E Company even acquired three German machine guns.[10] Part of their training had been devoted to learning to operate enemy weapons. All those grueling weeks of torturous exercises was paying off.

* * * *

Unit: Company D
Location: Kerchner's position

A lack of food and water also troubled the men. Kerchner knew no supplies would be arriving any time soon. After deploying the 20 D Company men, Lieutenant Kerchner and a few of his men turned their attention to procuring some food. Like the other Rangers, they had not eaten since 3:00 a.m. that morning. It was now around 8:00 p.m. or 9:00 p.m. He tried to force down the horrible D-ration chocolate bars, but it was impossible. The men needed real food, and they needed water. Kerchner spotted a tent 40 to 50 yards away from his command post. Taking several men with him, they carefully made their way to the area. The place was in shambles, surrounded by bodies of their fallen enemy. The lieutenant found a chunk of black bread. He divided it among the men who were with him. It was hard, but to the starving Americans it tasted wonderful. Kerchner also took some cigars he found there; he thought they might find a use for them later.[11] Shoving the cigars in his pocket, the lieutenant and his men returned to their position behind the hedgerow.

Twilight deepened into a solemn darkness around 11:30 p.m. It was almost a full moon, but visibility was poor to the front of Company D. Hundreds of trees in the orchards cast dark shadows making most of the area pitch black. Everything was very quiet. No fighting had occurred for several hours. "We were beginning to relax and feel that the war was almost over, for us, anyway, and very shortly the friendly troops were going to come up [from Omaha Beach], and we were going to go back to England. We had accomplished our D-Day mission." Kerchner's perception of the situation was shattered when a high shrieking whistle broke the deceptively calm silence.

The Liberation of Pointe du Hoc

A flare flew up into the night sky; hordes of Germans let loose blood-curdling yells and hurled grenades. They had crept to within 50 or 75 yards of the Rangers' position. The young lieutenant recalled the first moments of the attack:

> . . . Well this was the most frightening moment of my entire life — from being completely quiet and solemn . . . to this tremendous firing . . . going on, grenades bursting, flares, men yelling, whistles blowing, and it just seemed like there were hundreds and hundreds of Germans running towards us.[12]

German machine guns blasted D and E Companies' perimeter corner; tracers flew by Sergeant Branley and Pfc. Carty's position. Branley called out above the pall of battle, "Carty, we got to get the hell out of here!" The two headed back to D Company's main position. A grenade burst near Carty, and he fell dead. Sgt. Michael Branley suffered a bullet wound in the shoulder, but he made it back to the D Company hedgerow line.

The Germans concentrated their fire near Kerchner's position. Sgt. Harry J. Fate was with the lieutenant at the angle. The lieutenant felt he should move to the center of D Company's line where most of the men were grouped. Lieutenant Kerchner yelled to Fate, "Look, this is what we're going to do. We're going to get all the men together, and we're going to pull out of our line and go around and make an attack in the rear of the Germans."

Kerchner and Fate took off. The lieutenant carried his rifle, pistol, and a bandolier of ammunition. He forgot his cartridge belt with his canteen, D-ration bars, extra ammo, and his cigarettes. The two made their way north toward the black-top highway. Kerchner called out to his men along the hedgerow, "I want you to follow me, and we're going to go up here, and we're going to go around and attack them from the rear."

The two Rangers jumped into one of the fox holes; 1st Sergeant Lomell met them. Lieutenant Kerchner was rattled and nervous; Lomell tried to calm down his commanding officer. "You don't know how many or where they are," he shouted above the noise of battle. Kerchner listened and rested for a bit. The lieutenant agreed with his trusted sergeant. D Company would hold out and keep the western flank secure as Lieutenant Colonel Rudder had directed him.[13]

* * * *

Unit: Company E
Location: Hedgerow line just south of the black-top highway

To the left of D Company's area, Company E Rangers sighted another machine gun about 50 yards away from their defensive line. The B.A.R. men returned fire, emptying their clips in one burst. Sgt. Robert A. Honhart and T/5 Leroy S. Thompson, armed with a B.A.R., had been stationed 75 yards south of Lieutenant Leagans' main line.

The Germans had almost walked over the advanced listening post. Thompson's keen eye-sight and alertness spotted the enemy silhouettes. He blasted the Germans;

three went down; the others dove for cover. Pinned down, the enemy soldiers released grenades. One exploded right in front of Thompson's face; he yelled out in pain. Sergeant Honhart saw blood rushing down his friend's face; the grenade had cut him badly. Thompson handed the B.A.R. to Honhart; they had to get out of there. Slowly, they made their way to E Company's hedgerow line.

Sergeant Honhart approached Lieutenant Kerchner's vacated defensive position. Honhart called out "Rupinski!" No one answered so Honhart hollered louder, "Rupinski, Rupinski!" With no reply, Honhart decided to make their way up to the black-top road. They passed directly in front of the hedgerow occupied by D Company without realizing their presence to reach the highway. From there they headed back to the cliff perimeter (see map 11).[14]

* * * *

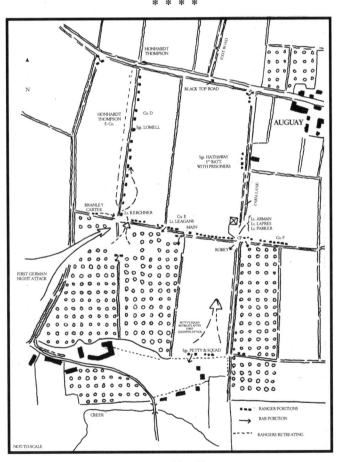

Map 11

June 6, first night counterattack, 11:30 p.m. Advance perimeter of 2d and 5th Ranger Battalions and the direction of the first night counterattack. The Germans focus their attention on D and E Companies' line. Sergeant Branley and Pfc. Carty withdraw; Kerchner and Fate retreat but reposition farther up D Company's line; Sergeant Honhart and T/5 Thompson are overwhelmed and retreat to the black-top highway. Shortly thereafter Sergeant Petty, F Company, returns to the hedgerow line.

Notes to Chapter 14

[1] Lisko's testimony.

[2] Chapelie, Lisko's testimony, 143-144.

[3] Chapelie, Hodenfield's testimony, 165.

[4] Chapelie, Lisko's testimony 144. See also Lane, 148.

[5] Len Lomell, notes to the author, July 29, 1999.

[6] Lane, 149. See also Kerchner, 26.

[7] Lane 128 and 143.

[8] Len Lomell, notes to the author, August 13, 1999.

[9] Kerchner, 26-27.

[10] *Small Unit Actions,* 53.

[11] Kerchner, 27-28.

[12] *Ibid.,* 28.

[13] *Small Unit Actions,* 52-54; Kerchner, 29-30, and Kerchner, diary, 7. See also Lane, 151-153. Lomell, notes to author, July 29, 1999.

[14] *Small Unit Actions,* 54-55. See also, Lane, 152.

Chapter 15

"My God, There's Guys Gettin' Killed Everywhere!":
Second and Third Counterattacks - June 7

Unit: Company F
Location: Left flank of roadblock position

Since the enemy assault had zeroed in on D Company's sector and the right flank of E Company's position, Company E's first platoon and Company F, over on the left flank, did not take part in the action of the first assault. Sergeant Petty's men heard the intense firing and explosions, but they could not see any German soldiers. They did not know what was happening, but the noise of battle soon died down.

With the attack discontinued, silence returned. Petty remained alert and listened. Noises could be heard from some farm buildings positioned to his right front. Seconds later a machine gun opened on Petty's outpost. The Rangers dove for cover but did not shoot back. The Germans mysteriously ceased firing.

Sergeant Petty decided it was high time to return to the hedgerow defensive line. The men quietly made their way back and safely repositioned themselves. Five of Petty's men deployed to the east of Lapres' and Arman's Headquarters. Sergeant Petty, still carrying his B.A.R., and Pfc. Frederick A. Dix, armed with a machine gun, took up positions in front of the command post.

Arman, at his Headquarters, was not informed that Kerchner had left his position. Since the first attack had come from the south-west, Lieutenant Arman considered moving Company F down to the creek and realigning on a north-south line. Arman, however, abandoned this idea. The potential for firing into other Rangers was too great.

While Arman agonized over their situation, and Petty returned to the main line, Lieutenant Lapres, Company E, and two other sergeants walked up and down F Company's line and directed the men to stay alert. A painful, nervous anxiety, a longing for action overwhelmed the Rangers. Fighting was better than waiting, anything to occupy their attention — a dull feeling about their chests made breathing difficult and painful. All energies of their souls seemed concentrated in their one desire for action. The enemy would return.[1]

* * * *

Unit: Company D
Location: Right flank

A tense hour passed without any detection of enemy movement. Sgt. Michael Branley and T/5 Henry S. Stecki occupied the vacated corner position of D Company's line. The Rangers waited with extreme tension, and the cord must soon snap one way or the other.

Around 1:00 a.m. whistles broke the silence again; flares lit up the night sky and yells resounded from the orchard.[2] Without being detected, the Germans had once again crept to within several yards of the American position. Like the first night assault, the second one came from the direction of the orchard just west of D Company's line and centered at the angle.

Tracers and machine gun bullets danced all around Sergeants Branley and Stecki; 75mm mortars and grenades exploded. Stecki returned fire with his B.A.R.; the glow of the blasts gave away his position, and the Germans lobbed grenades in his direction. Shrapnel and dirt knocked T/5 Stecki down; his post fell silent.

Shaking off the concussion, Stecki resumed the fight. More grenades landed near him and burst. This time he was knocked completely unconscious; the enemy infiltrated the American perimeter and captured Stecki, Sgt. Emory Jones and Sgt. Richard McLaughlin. S/Sgt. Lawrence Johnson was killed during the assault. The Germans had seized and occupied the corner position.[3]

Rushing through the angle, the antagonists were now in the rear of the Ranger line. The second counterattack was so swift that the G.I.s on the flanks did not realize what had happened. Meanwhile, the fighting subsided as the Germans reorganized for a third attack.

* * * *

Unit: Company E and F
Location: Command post of Companies E and F
Neither the D Company Rangers to the west or the Companies E and F men to the east realized their precarious situation. Darkness covered the German breakthrough.

At Companies E and F command post officers thought they heard enemy voices in their rear, but they sent no patrols to check it out. Hearing and seeing no D Company men or weapons, Lieutenant Lapres, Company E, and Arman, Company F, mistakenly concluded that Company D had withdrawn.

"I think they've been overrun." Lapres told Arman.

Lieutenant Arman agreed, "Yeah, I know. And the Krauts were yelling behind us. I think maybe they broke through an' have us cut off!"

But the shouting could have come from German prisoners. The two men were not sure; however, Arman felt if there was a follow-up assault, he would have to withdraw Companies E and F's line.[4]

* * * *

Unit: Company E
Location: Center of roadblock line
While Lieutenants Arman and Lapres discussed their options, the men deployed behind the hedgerow struggled to stay awake. It was now about 3:00 a.m., June 7. Most of the Rangers had been up for 24 hours; they had climbed the cliffs and fought their way to the black-top highway. They needed sleep; heads began to nod.

The Rangers were jolted awake at 3:00 a.m. when whistles and shouting disrupted the silence for a third time. This time, however, the Germans concentrated their assault on Company E's area. They had set up a machine gun at Kerchner's old position and sent a murderous flanking fire straight down E Company's line right to the command post. The roar of this sudden, blinding, raking volley was like the crack of doom.

Seconds later enemy infantrymen rushed the Ranger position. Pfc. George H. Crook, Company E, fired point blank into the onrushing Germans. They returned fire; Crook fell dead. In a nearby foxhole, a grenade seriously wounded Pfc. Harold D. Main; he heard German voices approaching, and he hid in a thicket of vines and briars.

Main could hear Sergeant Simmons only 15 feet away from him. After expending his ammunition, S/Sgt. Curtis A. Simmons, with German rifles pointing at him, dropped his weapon and threw his hands up. The enemy infantrymen refrained from shooting their captive. Germans then found and captured Pfc. Harold Main.

To the right of Simmons' foxhole the German machine gun fire pinned down T/5 John S. Burnett. Burnett, however, threw grenades from his prone position. Earlier he had collected discarded German grenades, and now he used them freely. In the midst of the commotion, he realized Sgt. Domenick Bogetto's B.A.R. had gone silent.

A sheet of German fire enfiladed his flank; Burnett went down wounded. As he lay on the ground he heard S/Sgt. Frank A. Rupinski arguing with other Rangers about continuing the battle or surrendering. The enemy was on three sides of them, and Rupinski felt it would be suicidal to continue. He then shouted, "*Kamerad! Kamerad!*" The Germans stopped firing and rounded up their prisoners.[5] About 20 Rangers were captured, nearly all of Leagans' 2d Platoon, Company E. Lieutenant Leagans was killed in the assault.

Pfc. Salva Maimone escaped capture. He recalled the vicious fire fights in the early morning hours of June 7. "Every time we'd shoot, they'd come back with more fire. They had lots of mortar shells going into the position where they thought we were; but we weren't there."[6]

* * * *

Unit: Companies E and F
Location: Command post inland

Pfc. Maimone and those E Company boys who had survived the latest attack were compelled to withdraw under pressure of the German assault. Arman and Lapres at their command post did not have time to issue a formal order. But when the officers heard the third assault begin, they knew it was time to get out.

Adding support to their decision, one Ranger from Company E ran into the command post and frantically shouted, "The Germans have broken through. We couldn't hold 'em, Lieutenant. My God, there's guys gettin' killed everywhere!" The Ranger also wrongly claimed that D Company had been wiped out.

T/5 Edward J. Smith and T/5 Charles H. Dunlap entered the command post because their guns had jammed. They reported to Arman that "there [were] no Rangers left between Lieutenant Leagans and . . . [their] position. I don't know where they went!"[7]

According to plan or not, a full retreat was occurring in Companies E and F. Many of F Company had already taken off, and the survivors of E Company headed north toward Rudder's perimeter back at the bluff. Arman and the officers remained in their command post.

The Liberation of Pointe du Hoc

* * * *

Unit: Company F
Location: North-east corner of wheatfield — just south of Arman's command post

Immediately prior to the general retreat of E and F Companies, Sergeant Petty, armed with his B.A.R., and S/Sgt. Frederick A. Dix, carrying a German machine gun, with a few F Company riflemen, reinforced the north-east corner of a wheatfield (see map 12).

Dix spotted a German squad coming from the east and entering a farm lane. When they were only a few feet away, Sergeant Dix attempted to fire his weapon. The captured German machine gun jammed. At the same time a bullet fired by a Ranger shooting down the lane glanced off Dix's helmet. A bit stunned, Dix started to creep back to Arman's command post.

Sergeant Petty suddenly shouted, "Down!" Dix hit the dirt; Petty blasted the Germans coming up the lane; Sergeant Robey joined in with his B.A.R. Most of the enemy soldiers were killed or scattered. One German managed to crawl along the hedgerow into Arman's command post. A Ranger lobbed a grenade; it landed under the chest of the soldier and blew him apart. For now, the German attack had been stalled.

Enemy fire, however, continued to come from across the wheatfield in the west. The volume soon picked up again; Arman realized the Germans were renewing their assault. Men on both sides were falling, either dead or wounded, like leaves from the trees, until it seemed to be only a question of little time until they would entirely destroy each other. Lieutenant Arman sent a hasty and informal message to anyone remaining to make their way back to the black-top highway. Sergeants Petty and Robey were ordered to cover their withdrawal.

* * * *

5th Rangers
Location: North of Arman's command post — about halfway between his headquarters and the black-top road near the lane

Once the retreat had begun, movement was fast. S/Sgt. Richard N. Hathaway, 5th Rangers, had been stationed north of and halfway between the black-top highway and Arman's command post. He and several other 5th Rangers guarded some of the German prisoners.

A few of the slightly wounded Rangers had become panic-stricken; it was dark, and the enemy was everywhere. Hathaway saw the 2d Rangers heading north on the farm lane. He stuck his head through the hedgerow and asked them, "Hey! What's up? Where you going?"

Bereft of reason, not realizing it was a fellow American, the nearest Ranger going up the lane stopped; he pointed his rifle in Hathaway's face demanding the password. Sergeant Hathaway momentarily froze; fear drove the word from his mind. Just in time, he spewed it out.

The crazed Ranger then shouted, "The Germans are right behind us — get out quick to the Pointe!" Sergeant Hathaway quickly assembled his men. They abandoned their prisoners and headed north toward the Pointe.[8]

* * * *

Unit: Company D
Location: Right flank of inland position

Unknown to Company E and F Rangers, D Company was still manning their position on the right flank. Lieutenant Kerchner, Company D, explained the situation:

> . . . the . . . attack overran the position held by E company and part of F company. These two companies decided that they couldn't hold . . . and they decided to withdraw . . . we didn't know that they were pulling out. We were over in the right dug in this hedgerow. So the Germans made one more attack, and then found out that they had captured the position. E and F had gone; they didn't know we were in this hedgerow which was heavily overgrown with under brush and deep holes.[9]

Kerchner and the D Company men were alone and surrounded by Germans, but due to the darkness and terrain, the predators did not realize that the Rangers were still there. The men were cut off from each other, hunkered down in holes covered by heavy brush. None of the D Company survivors knew how many friendly troops held on. The two boat teams, which had numbered approximately 44 strong, had been reduced to about 14 men. Directly deployed behind the hedgerow line were Kerchner, Lomell, Kuhn, Arthur, Huff, Hoover, Fate, Flanagan, Austin, Sweany and Branley; the latter was badly wounded.[10]

The foliage provided cover only and was no protection from deadly missiles; yet, their survival instincts and months of training kept them from panicking. Although frightened, no one made any sudden movements or breathed too loudly to give away their position.

The three D Company Rangers sent by 1st Sergeant Lomell to the roadblock area remained there - cut off from Kerchner's and Lomell's hedgerow line (see map 12).

* * * *

Units: Company F, a few E Company and 5th Ranger platoon
Location: Black-top highway

At the highway, Lieutenant Arman, Company F, conducted a quick check of who had made it. Most of F Company were accounted for, but Company E only had a few survivors. Lieutenant Arman split the men into two groups. He sent the first party east and then north toward the Pointe. Arman, with the second group, retreated back to Rudder's command post via the exit road. The 5th Ranger platoon's point scout followed Lieutenant Arman's group and traversed the unfamiliar terrain in the darkness. The Rangers estimated that approximately 300 Germans participated in the 3 counterattacks.[11]

The Liberation of Pointe du Hoc

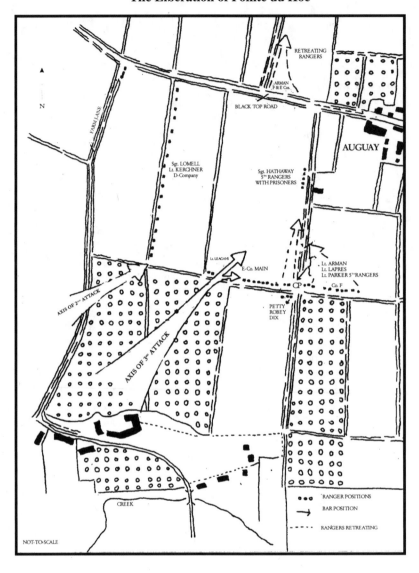

Map 12
June 7, 3:30-4:00 a.m.
Petty and other F Company men deploy in the north-east corner of a wheatfield; they hold back a German assault. Arman gives the word to withdrawal. S/Sergeant Hathaway, 5th Rangers, encounters a 2d Ranger. Companies E and F and 1st Platoon, Company A, 5th Rangers retreat to the black-top road and then back to the Pointe. Kerchner's and Lomell's Company D men remain at their hedgerow defensive position. Three Rangers from D Company also hold out at the roadblock on the black-top road.

Notes to Chapter 15

[1] Lane, 153-154.
[2] Chapelie, Hodenfield's testimony, 165.
[3] *Small Unit Actions,* 56-57. See also Kerchner's diary, pg. 8.
[4] First hand account by Lapres. See also Lane 155 and *Small Unit Actions,* 57.
[5] *Small Actions,* 58.
[6] Drez, account by Salva Maimone, 265.
[7] *Small Unit Actions,* 58-59.
[8] *Ibid.,* 59-60.
[9] Kerchner, 30.
[10] Kerchner's diary, 9.
[11] Interview with Len Lomell, August 21, 1999.

Chapter 16

"I Gave Up Hope of Getting Off Pointe du Hoc Alive":
June 7, 3:30 a.m.-7:00 a.m.

Unit: Headquarters
Location: Rudder's command post

When the third attack began farther inland, the Rangers in Rudder's command post could hear the intensity of the fighting. The situation seemed grim. Journalist G. K. Hodenfield later wrote:

> . . . I gave up hope of getting off Pointe du Hoc alive. No reinforcements in sight, plenty of Germans in front of us, nothing behind us but sheer cliffs and [the] Channel . . . Most of our men, in order to carry more ammunition, had left their canteens and rations in the supply boat which was to have followed us in, but that supply boat, it turned out, was one of the first boats sunk. Without our supply boat, we were up the creek not only for food and water but also for ammunition.[1]

Around 4:00 a.m. about 50 men safely from E and F Companies returned to the Pointe. Lieutenant Colonel Rudder had been mistakenly informed that D Company was destroyed, but he now realized that E Company had been nearly wiped out. Rudder deployed the 50 survivors into a hastily placed defensive line from gun position No. 6 to gun emplacement No. 4. At this point, there were only about 90 Rangers guarding the cliff. The assailants could have easily recaptured the Pointe. Fortunately for the Rangers, the Germans did not follow up their attack.[2]

* * * *

Unit: Company F and E
Location: Petty and Robey's withdrawal

The majority of Rangers who returned safely to the crest of the cliff owed their lives to Sergeant Petty, Company F, and Sergeant Robey, Company E. Both were armed with B.A.R.s and had been assigned to cover Companies F and E's retreat.

After their comrades had pulled out, the two sergeants began to follow using leap-frog tactics. Petty blasted the Germans as Robey ran 30 yards rearward; Sergeant Robey then took cover and discharged his B.A.R. while Petty withdrew and joined him. During their second move, however, Petty became separated from Robey.

The Germans continued to advance through the wheatfield toward Robey's position. Believing Petty had been killed or captured, Robey decided to high tale it out of there. Now Sgt. Bill, "L-Rod", Petty, was alone behind enemy lines. Petty's survival instincts kicked in.

When the Germans came out in the open they were silhouetted in the moonlight. L-Rod let loose with his B.A.R. then immediately darted to a different position before the enemy could return fire. From another angle, the sergeant again sprayed automatic fire. Moving from ditch to ditch, tree to tree, he was able to confuse the Germans: How many Americans were out there? One, twenty, or more? This harassing fire slowed their pursuit on the main body of the remaining F and E Company Rangers.

After about an hour of dodging Germans, Petty arrived at the black-top highway. All of his comrades were long gone. But he spotted a column of enemy infantrymen near a hedgerow bordering the road. The sergeant slithered into a bomb crater, pointed his weapon and pulled the trigger. A burst of gun fire resounded; German soldiers fell dead or wounded; the survivors scattered.

Silence descended. The sergeant caught his breath and then zig-zagged to a nearby cottage. Bomb craters surrounded the house. Petty looked around; no one was in sight — friend or foe. Not wanting to give a sniper a perfect target, he took cover in one of the shell holes. Exhausted, he decided to remain here and wait for other American units coming from Omaha Beach to hook up with Rudder's Rangers. As he waited among the dead he dosed off.[3]

* * * *

Unit: Company F, Sgt. Bill Petty
Location: Moving quickly to the Pointe
Petty awoke at dawn to the sound of voices coming from the cottage. He jumped up and out of the shell hole; he thought American units had reached the Pointe and had entered the house.

When he came within ear shot of the farm house, however, he heard the men inside speaking German. He quickly turned and began sprinting toward the Pointe. The enemy soldiers never saw the sergeant. Sergeant Petty continued his trek to the cliff; he did not know if any Rangers had survived, but he hoped he'd bump into some Americans soon; being alone and surrounded by the enemy took a toll on one's nerves.

As he serpentined through the crater-filled terrain, he looked up and saw the backs of Germans firing at the cliff. The 2d Battalion shot back; a few stray American bullets came terrifyingly close to Petty. He was elated to discover that Rangers were still alive at the Pointe. Without hesitation, Petty blasted the Germans from the rear, ran through their line, and sprinted across the battle zone. Pfc. Carl Winsch, Company F, spotted him and shouted to the other Rangers, "Don't shoot — Don't shoot, that's L-Rod!"

His Company F buddies were glad to see that their tough sergeant was still alive. Capt. Masny walked over to Petty and offered him half of a chocolate bar. It wasn't much, but the sergeant was starved and accepted it gladly. Sgt. Bill Petty was credited with killing 30 enemy soldiers from June 6-8. As L-Rod had promised Lieutenant Colonel Rudder as a new recruit, he had fought the Germans with courage and initiative, and he would continue to do so.

* * * *

Unit: Headquarters
Location: Command Post near the cliff

Dawn of June 7 revealed the huge armada of ships lying off the Normandy coast. Corporal Lisko vividly recalled seeing the destroyers *Satterlee* and the *U.S.S. Harding*, pummeling German positions. The enemy artillery returned fire, but the Allied ships held their positions close to the shore.[4] It was quite an encouraging sight for young Lisko.

* * * *

Unit: Company D
Location: South of the black-top highway behind a hedgerow

While Lisko watched the artillery duel at the cliff, Lieutenant Kerchner and about 15 D Company Rangers remained hidden behind the hedgerow line. They did not hear or see any other G.I. soldiers. The men realized they were stranded a mile inland and behind enemy lines. Company F and the few surviving Rangers from E Company had withdrawn at 3:30 a.m., June 7. But D Company had not received any orders to retreat, and they had not been "duly relieved." Using their survival training they dug in and hid in the thick hedgerow; they lay waiting for any Germans foolish enough to test their tenacity; tension ran high.

Early on June 7, Kerchner heard rustling in a nearby ditch that ran through the hedgerow in which he was hiding. He told the story:

> . . . Of course, I was scared. I figured it was the Germans digging us out. I was all set to try and defend myself when I realized they were Americans — two Americans from E Company that had been left behind . . . So we were the only ones out there in this field. I think there were fifteen of us. These two men from E company came in and joined us and they got in the hole with me . . . .[5]

Fortunately for the lieutenant the two men had water and some D-bars. Kerchner could only contribute the cigars he had found, but he had no matches. They shared what little they had and remained in the fox hole.

Germans occupied the fields to D Company's front and rear, and the lieutenant felt it was unwise to try and fight their way out. There were approximately 100 Germans all around, and the 15 or so men of Company D were outnumbered by about 10-1; but because of the thick underbrush and hedgerows the Rangers could only spot about three or four enemy soldiers at a time. No additional U.S. infantrymen were sighted, but they watched as an American tank tried to get through. German artillery zeroed in on the tank, and it was forced to withdraw.

Miles away the Battleship *Texas* sighted the enemy artillery unit; her huge 14 inch guns opened on the battery situated near the field in which D Company was hiding. Some shells landed within 50 yards of Kerchner's men. Lieutenant Kerchner recalled the terrifying experience:

> . . . where a shell would land it would dig a hole 15-20 feet in diameter and 4 or 5 feet deep. You could imagine what a noise it made when it went off and of course you didn't know where the

next one was going to land either . . . I can say that I had a prayer book in my pocket. I'm a Roman Catholic. I did a tremendous amount of praying when I was in that ditch. I read that prayer book through from cover to cover, I suppose, a half dozen times, and I prayed very sincerely for [protection] and actually it's not apropos, but since then I feel so guilty at all the things I asked for on D-Day and what I asked the Lord to do for me, which was primarily to get me out of there alive. I've been ashamed to ask for anything since then. I figured I used up all I had coming to me on D-Day.[6]

Miraculously, D Company made it through the barrage of artillery fire. The Battleship ceased firing when the sun set, and all was quiet.

* * * *

Notes to Chapter 16

[1] Chapelie, Hodenfield's testimony, 166.
[2] *Small Unit Actions,* 61.
[3] Lane, 162-163.
[4] Chapelie, Lisko's testimony, 146.
[5] Kerchner, 30-31.
[6] *Ibid.,* 31-32. See also Kerchner's diary, 10-12.

Chapter 17

"The Rangers Were Still Alive":
Afternoon-Evening, June 7

Unit: Headquarters Company
Location: Command Post near the cliff

At Headquarters the men were busy gathering prisoners and scrounging up ammunition and weapons. One Ranger guarded about 10 captives in a bomb crater to the right of the command post. An American helping a wounded comrade reach Doc Block's aid station walked passed these prisoners. The wounded man recognized a German soldier who had killed his friend. Although injured, the Ranger went mad; he grabbed for a machine gun and was going to kill the prisoner. Cpl. Lou Lisko and several other Headquarters men ran to put a stop to this action. They brought the crazed man, who was by now in shock, to the medical station.

After leaving the soldier at Doc's makeshift hospital, Lisko and the other men saw American fighter planes circling the Pointe. The soldiers became alarmed, thinking that the pilots might mistake the Rangers for Germans. Corporal Lisko recalled the tense scene:

> . . . Then immediately everybody in the Command Post stood up. I had my field jacket and started to wave it at the planes. One came down very close, so close that the roar of the motors was hard on my eardrums. Someone had an American flag and started to stretch it, putting some stones on it so that the wind would not blow it away. The [German] machine gun on the left flank started to fire at the ranger; he fell back down but was not hit, then he crawled back up again to put some more stones on the flag. This gave the leader of the flight . . . a chance to see the rangers were still alive. His plane flew in a circle a couple of times. We waved at him, and he waved back.[1]

Discovering that the soldiers were Rangers, the seven American planes headed back to England.

Hours later, three or four planes returned and pulverized a German machine gun nest on the left flank. At least six to eight bombs were dropped; no harassing fire was heard from this position again.

While the Allied Navy and Army Air Corps aided in destroying some enemy sites, they could not drop or bring in needed supplies. The Rangers rationed food, water and ammunition. To help ease the ammo and weapons shortage they used captured or discarded German weapons. At one point, Pvt. Lester Zages, of Detroit, ran into the command post yelling excitedly, "Dammit! I got eight of 'em already and with one of their own guns, too!"[2]

Small arms weren't the only weapons emancipated; Rudder's men took a German machine gun and set it up right in front of the command post. The Headquarters' men not busy with their formal duties were assigned to find and gather mortar and rifle shells. To the young Rangers, their situation still seemed grim. Their backs

The Liberation of Pointe du Hoc

Taken around noon June 8, 1944 by the U.S. Army Signal Corps.
When American planes circled the Pointe on June 7, the Rangers placed an American flag near Rudder's command post. Lieutenant Colonel Rudder is standing at the top of the cliff watching German prisoners being brought in by members of the 5th Rangers Battalion. Cpl. Lou Lisko (facing the camera) is sitting at the bottom left corner with his back to a concrete slab. Lisko Ranger Box, USAMHI

On the 35th Anniversary of D-Day, June 6, 1979, Lou Lisko returned to the Pointe. He sits in the exact spot in which he was photographed on June 8, 1944. Lisko Ranger Box, USAMHI

were to the sea; the Germans surrounded them and even scurried like rats in tunnels below them. Food and water were low, and most of the ammunition had been expended. Yet, through all this, Lt. Col. James Rudder seemed cool and calm, master of the situation.

The colonel maintained contact with patrols via radios; he checked on the wounded, and he continued to strengthen his defenses. Sometime in the afternoon, Captain Masny reported to Rudder that he had located a German ammunition dump. The captain assured his commander that the site could be blown with a four-man patrol and some bangalore torpedoes.

* * * *

Unit: Company F
Location: German Ammo dump behind the enemy lines
Lieutenant Hodenfield overheard Masny's and Rudder's conversation and mentioned that he would like a safe vantage point from which to view the spectacle. Before the eager lieutenant realized what was happening, Captain Masny was handing him a bangalore torpedo. Hodenfield did not know how to back out of this one so he followed the captain. Masny picked two other men to accompany them: Lt. Elmer "Dutch" Vermeer, Engineer and demolition officer, and Pvt. William F. "Andy" Anderson. Private Anderson hated Germans and was always enthusiastic about taking them out.[3]

Since the area was behind the lines, Sergeant Petty and other Rangers from F Company covered Masny's advance. The captain and his three cohorts slipped through the line. Petty followed them closely to provide additional protection. Anderson took a bangalore torpedo and slid it inside the doors of the little building that held the explosives. The private lit the fuse and the party "high tailed it out of there" with Hodenfield leading the race. A huge explosion shook the Pointe; great sheets of flame shot up from the ammo dump. Clouds of dirt, rifle shells and hunks of wood rained down on the crew. Masny's patrol ducked into an empty bunker to take cover from the falling debris.[4]

Inside they found Pfc. George Schneller, Company D, terribly wounded. He had been hit earlier on June 6 by a mortar shell which had torn a hole in his back. It was a sickening sight, and the men were surprised Schneller was still alive. When the dust and debris settled, Petty and Anderson attempted to carry him back to Doc's station. Capt. Otto Masny, a big man and an impatient one, walked back and picked Schneller up, single-handedly carrying him back to the Pointe.[5]

* * * *

Unit: Headquarters
Location: Command Post
Back at the cliff, the men turned toward the sound of the explosion. They saw a huge dust cloud shoot into the air and then settle back down to earth. The German's precious supply of ammo had been depleted. To further boost their morale, late in the afternoon an LST, commanded by Maj. Jack Street, landed and took away the wounded men and prisoners. Major Street then moved his craft to Omaha Beach and

rounded up about twenty 5th Rangers and brought them to the Pointe. They brought with them needed supplies.[6]

* * * *

Location: Cliff perimeter

That evening Doc Block made jam sandwiches. To the hungry Rangers it was a deluxe meal. Their stomachs full, to their delight, the Germans did not counterattack that evening of June 7-8th, and the men were able to obtain a satisfied and much-needed rest. Exhausted, Hodenfield lay down at 2:00 a.m. The lieutenant commented, " . . . It was fairly quiet when I lay down to sleep...and it is a commentary on how tired a person can be that I slept soundly for six hours, with a sharp rock digging into the center of my spine."[7]

* * * *

Unit: Company D
Location: South of the black-top highway

After the big guns of the Battleship *Texas* stopped, Kerchner remained in his foxhole all night — awake with his pistol in one hand and a grenade in the other. Trapped in their positions, some D Company Rangers were forced to use their helmets for toilets. This rendered many of the men helmetless for the time being. Still on full alert, the men took turns resting. A few, however, did not sleep at all but kept a continuous watch over the situation. In Kerchner's sector no Germans were heard or seen that night.[8]

Notes to Chapter 17

[1] Chapelie, Lisko's testimony, 147.
[2] Chapelie, Hodenfield's testimony, 166.
[3] Anderson was later killed at Hill 400, December, 1944.
[4] Hodenfield's testimony, 167.
[5] Lane, 165.
[6] Ambrose, 416. See also Hodenfield, 168-169. Major Street had been with the 1st Rangers but was now attached to the U.S. Navy.
[7] Hodenfield, 169.
[8] Kerchner, 33, and diary,12. For the use of the helmets as toilets — taken from telephone conversation with Jack E. Kuhn, July 11, 1999.

Chapter 18

The Liberation of Pointe du Hoc:
D-Day +2

Unit: Company D
Location: Inland, black-top highway

When Lieutenant Kerchner still did not sight any Germans the next morning he assumed, and rightfully so, that the terrible pummeling by the ship's big guns had chased the enemy from the area. The lieutenant was fed up with being cooped up in a ditch with two other men. He decided to find out what was going on. His entire body ached from lying in a cramped position for more than 24 hours, and he was weak from lack of food and water. The lieutenant made his way down the hedgerow to see if any of his men had weathered the fire storm.

Going from hole to hole, to his delight Kerchner found that 12 of his men were still alive; two of them were wounded. The lieutenant also found several of his men dead. Equipment was strewn everywhere. All the D Company soldiers had been separated and had not known the outcome for E and F Companies. Everyone was glad to see their buddies. Several times, however, Kerchner startled his men as he crashed through the hedgerow.

Sgts. Jack Kuhn and Harry Fate shared a foxhole. On the morning of the 8th they heard a tank and men running. 1st Sergeant Lomell of the 2d Platoon also noted the sounds of tanks and surmised they were coming from Omaha Beach (east). Kuhn and Fate thought this was the end; the Germans were rushing their position. The two sergeants pointed their weapons ready to go down fighting and take as many of the enemy with them as they could.

Fortunately, just before they pulled the trigger, they identified Lieutenant Kerchner coming through the hedgerow calling out, "Hey, is everybody all right?" They lowered their pieces, gave a sigh of relief, and joined the survivors of D Company.[1]

Unlike Kuhn and Fate, when Sgt. Michael Branley saw his lieutenant he almost kissed him. Kerchner noted Branley's bandaged shoulder, but his sergeant was alive. Reunited, the weary band decided to walk back and find out if any other Americans were out there. Several yards east, on the black-top road, they saw a column of U.S. troops coming up the highway; they were overjoyed. Lieutenant Kerchner recalled the scene vividly:

> . . . right up behind the lead scouts was Col. Canham who was the commander of the 116th infantry . . . Col. Canham came up this road with one hand bandaged up. He had been wounded...we were so glad to see him. Col. Canham was all soldier, and all he wanted to know was, 'Where are the Germans?' and all I wanted to know was, 'Where are the Americans?' at this stage.[2]

These were the reinforcements the Rangers had been waiting for and Colonel Charles Canham's 116th Inf. Regt., 29th Inf. Div., "duly relieved" D Company.

The Liberation of Pointe du Hoc

Lomell's 2d Platoon and Kerchner's 1st Platoon, had kept their roadblock on the western flank for 2 1/2 days. They had cut German communication lines, destroyed the big guns, and, although outnumbered, they and Companies E and F had prevented German reinforcements from getting through to Omaha Beach or to the Pointe. D Company, 1st and 2d Platoon's efforts, however, did not come without great cost. In two days they suffered the highest casualties of any other unit at Pointe-du-Hoc — 17 men were killed in action and many more were wounded.

While the remnants of D Company were glad to see the 116th, Kerchner could not tell Canham much. He had been stuck in a ditch for more than a day, out of touch with the main body of 2d Rangers. At this moment the lieutenant wasn't even sure Rudder and the others had survived. The last time Kerchner had heard from the colonel he was still at his command post on the Pointe, but hours had passed since then and there was no telling what may have happened in the interim.

As they were discussing the whereabouts of the enemy, they turned their attention toward the Pointe and the sound of gun fire.

* * * *

Unit: Headquarters Company
Location: Rudder's command post, cliff perimeter

The men on the Pointe awoke on June 8 to German artillery fire. Each hour grew more tense. There was no sign of the 5th Ranger Battalion, or Companies A, B, C, 2d Rangers, or the 116th Infantry Regiment. Corporal Lisko and his fellow Rangers hoped and prayed the American force from Omaha Beach would reach their position before the Germans made another counterattack. Only a handful of Rangers were left. Out of the 225 men who landed, only 90 were still alive. Ammunition was running low, and weapons were scarce. Two Americans were manning a German machine gun which had been captured.

Around noon, Lt. Col. Max Schneider, with the 5th Battalion, approached the perimeter from the east (left). Schneider heard the unique sound of an M.G. 42 enemy machine gun near the cliff. Rudder's Rangers were firing the captured weapon at some unidentified object, but the lieutenant colonel and his men thought the 2d Ranger Battalion had been wiped out. In the confusion, the 5th Rangers started to lob mortars into the perimeter line. Tanks from the 116th Inf. Regt. soon joined the attack. Rudder's men had endured two days of German onslaughts, and now they were in danger of being killed by friendly fire.

Lieutenant Colonel Rudder directed his men to stop firing the captured piece, but they were too far away to hear him. Lisko and his fellow Headquarters comrades tried to radio the Allied contingency attacking them. Finally, T/5 Frank "Killer" Kolodziejczak, succeeded in reaching the 5th Rangers. Risking his own life, Schneider ran out in the open and ordered his men to stop firing. The fighting on the cliff was over. Pointe-du-Hoc had been liberated![3]

* * * *

Unit: Survivors of the 2d Ranger Battalion
Location: Cliff perimeter, moving away from the Pointe

The D Company survivors returned to the command post shortly after noon. Rudder was making preparations to join with the other American units; his men surrounded him listening and watching intently. They stood in the solitude, grim-faced relics of war.

Lt. Col. James Earl Rudder had led these young heroes through their first mission and, though wounded three times, he had remained on the field of battle. He chose to fight and die, if need be, as a Ranger.

As the colonel spoke with his men, Corporal Lisko chanced to glance out to sea. Thousands of ships and boats moved closer to shore and disgorged their supplies and personnel. The Invasion had been a success. Lisko's keen eyesight spotted a flashing signal light coming from the *Ellyson*. He politely interrupted Rudder and told him the ship was sending them a message. "What's the message?" Rudder asked. Corporal Lisko deciphered it: "We saw several of the enemy run into a barn, 3,000 yards to your right. May we fire on the barn?"

Lieutenant Colonel Rudder told Lisko to send back the reply, "no." There was a good possibility that there were U.S. troops in that area.

With this last message to the *Ellyson*, Lieutenant Colonel Rudder led his 2d

Lieutenant Colonel Rudder and his men gather at the Pointe.
The arrow points to Rudder. Directly in back of the colonel is Lieutenant Eikner; Sergeant Jack Kuhn is shown on the far left without his helmet and holding a Tommy gun. The soldier pointing is Sergeant Stinette, F Company, and the very large Ranger with his back to the camera, over on the right, is Captain "Big Stoop" Masny, F Company. Photo taken on June 8, '44. Ranger Signal Corps Box, USAMHI

The Liberation of Pointe du Hoc

With this last message to the *Ellyson*, Lieutenant Colonel Rudder led his 2d Rangers off the Pointe and toward the black-top highway. The earth was torn; shell craters marked the ground, clothes, empty ammo chests, canteens, discarded weapons, and hollow helmets were scattered throughout the area. The dead lay in contorted positions, mangled, dismembered, disemboweled, some torn literally to pieces: friend and foe alike. The memory of that barren field was burned into the minds of Corporal Lisko and his comrades .

> [It] was a very sad sight to see an American ranger that you had known lying on the battlefield, on a torn earth with dust and dirt all over his face, his body and his clothes, bullet holes here and there . . . I shall always remember the sight of a German. I guess he had tried to come out of a crater. As he came out a ranger hit him across the chest with a Tommy gun or a machine gun. He must have twisted and fell on his back. His head was lower than the rest of his body. He was there, lying, looking straight up with opened eyes; his face was a medium shade of blue because the blood had rushed to his head.[4]

Lt. Elmer "Dutch" Vermeer also recounted the departure of Rudder's Rangers:

> We left the area together, but the sounds and smells of the battlefield still remain vivid in my mind. Yes, you can see the battlefield and hear the battlefield, but it's the smell of death . . . . that really penetrates everything. You smell it as soon as the shells explode and the bullets fly, long before the dead bodies of your comrades start to decompose. It is a smell you'll never forget.[5]

The intense, melancholy scene was interrupted when the Rangers found a former German canteen on the Pointe. Upon investigation they found knives, razor blades and soap, and out back case after case of beer bottles stacked high. To everyone's disappointment they were all empty. Lt. Richard Wintz, F Company, exclaimed, "Now I really hate those Germans! Oh, how I hate those guys! They didn't even leave us a drink!"[6] With the canteen raid a bust, the men proceeded to the black-top highway.

* * * *

Unit: Headquarters Company
Location: Foxhole on the side of the highway

Once at the road there seemed to be less dead, and the men were ordered to dig foxholes along the hedgerow. While Corporal Lisko was digging he heard a jeep coming from Omaha Beach; he looked up from his task. The vehicle pulled to a stop by Lisko; the man sitting in the back seat, looking very impressive, stood up.[7]

"Are you a Ranger?" Brig. Gen. Norman Cota asked Lisko.

"Yes, sir, I am." Corporal Lisko replied.

Cota then inquired, "What happened to you men up here? It was a rough battle, wasn't it?"

Lisko again answered, "Yes."

"There were all kinds of conflicting reports about you guys. Some reports said the Rangers had landed and taken possession of the Pointe. Other reports stated the 2d Rangers had been wiped out, but another rumor came down that the Rangers were still fighting." General Cota provided a lengthy explanation of what he had heard about the battle for the Pointe.

The general then asked young Lisko where Lieutenant Colonel Rudder was; the corporal pointed in the direction of the new command post. Cota told his driver to move on, and the jeep sped away. Corporal Lisko and other 2d Rangers went back to digging their foxholes. Thinking about the conversation, he felt more secure seeing a general at the front line.[8]

Sniper fire and the battle for Grandcamp continued as the Rangers set up their defensive perimeter for the night. Near 9:00 p.m., the corporal jumped into his foxhole. All the men hoped for a good night's sleep, but Lisko was startled when he heard rifle fire. He sat up and peered out; two Rangers were shooting at two Germans running away from them.

The Americans had been escorting these prisoners to the rear when the Germans made a break for it. One fell on Lisko's side of the hedgerow; the other sprinted farther from the Rangers, but was finally hit. The escapee collapsed into a ditch. The man sat up, and one of the Rangers pumped two more bullets in his chest. Thinking the men were dead, the two Americans walked away.

Corporal Lisko watched and noticed that, miraculously, the man near his position was still moving. The wounded German brought his knee up and tried to get up after being shot four or five times. Lisko refused to go to sleep with an enemy soldier only ten yards from his foxhole. He shouted to the two Rangers, "He's not dead yet."

The Ranger who had shot the German, turned around, walked back and emptied his clip into the man's chest and back. He didn't move after that. Corporal Lisko commented on this gruesome scene. "This may sound like a cruel and inhuman thing to do, but these rangers were on the front line."[9] Lieutenant Kerchner, D Company, vividly described the psychology of a soldier in battle:

> . . . When you're actually fighting, when you're shooting at them and they're shooting at you, everyone of those men out there are your mortal enemy. You're just as anxious and trying hard to kill every single one of them. When the fighting would die down, you would think about it, especially when you saw the German prisoners come through, if you had been fighting hard and taking casualties, you were bitter toward them.[10]

After the shooting subsided in Lisko's area, he still could not rest. He was haunted by the grotesque forms of the dead German prisoners lying near his foxhole. Like Lisko, none of the 2d Rangers received a good night's sleep on June 8;

they were still on full alert. German resistance remained strong and fighting continued near Grandcamp. Exhausted, the men remained in their foxholes. No enemy attacks occurred on June 8, and the men had time to reflect upon their first mission, the friends they had left behind, and the battles still to be fought.[11]

* * * *

Location: Rudder's command post near the black-top highway

At Rudder's command post the colonel tallied his losses: 77 Rangers killed, 152 wounded and 38 missing — this number included Captain Slater's missing LCA and Companies A, B, C losses at Omaha Beach. Of the 225 men who actually landed and fought at Pointe-du-Hoc only 90 men remained.[12]

Rudder was proud of his men. They had punched through the formidable Nazi Atlantic Wall, destroyed the big guns, cut the German communications, and had held off five counterattacks. He knew his Rangers would have fought to the last man if he had asked them. He was glad he didn't have to.

Approximately 11 months of service lay ahead and many more battles, but Pointe-du-Hoc would always be remembered as their baptism by fire.

Notes to Chapter 18

[1] Kerchner, 33, and diary, 13.

[2] *Ibid.,* 33, and diary, 14-15.

[3] Chapelie, Lisko's testimony, 148-149.

[4] *Ibid.*

[5] Dutch Vermeer's oral history, Roland Rowe's Collection, 2d Ranger Battalion Box, USAMHI Archives.

[6] Chapelie, Hodenfield's testimony, 170.

[7] At the time Lou Lisko did not know that this officer was Brigadier General Cota of the 29th Inf. Div. He found this out later.

[8] Chapelie, Lisko's testimony 150.

[9] *Ibid.,* 151.

[10] Kerchner, 34.

[11] Since the 2d Rangers had suffered high casualties, the 116th Inf. Regt., 29th Inf. Div., moved ahead and captured the town of Grandcamp.

[12] Clark, 62. Phone conversation with James Eikner, July 25, 1999.

Chapter 19

Rudder's Rangers Were No More:
Conclusion

The liberation of Pointe-du-Hoc was the 2d Rangers' most celebrated battle, a textbook ranger-style mission, but the U.S. Army never again utilized the 2d Rangers to their fullest extent. Instead, they were assimilated into the 12th United States Army Group commanded by General Omar Bradley. Unlike the British commandos, who continued to be assigned covert action missions, the 2d Rangers were now used as line infantry. The American high command in Europe put more emphasis on the heavy infantry battalions.[1] Like a foster child shifted from one family to another, the 2d Rangers found themselves assigned and reassigned to various infantry divisions.

After resting, the battalion moved to Beaumont Hague on June 25th for the purpose of patrolling the Cherbourg Peninsula. This area was dangerous due to the heavy use of mine fields and booby traps. On July 19th the 2d Rangers were relieved and the rest of the month was spent in garrison. They were then attached to the 1st Army and left Beaumont Hague on August 6th. They arrived at Canissy on the 7th. Here the men trained in hedgerow fighting with the 159th Light Tank Battalion until August 10th. Once again ordered to move out, they arrived at Buais the next day and set up a defensive position on the high ground.

Their next large-scale campaign was in Brest. This action lasted from August 13 to September 8. After Brest, the 2d Battalion moved back to the rear line near Kervaiuen. On September 17, they were attached to the 8th Infantry Division and transported by truck to the vicinity of Crozon Peninsula which they helped to secure, freeing about 400 Allied prisoners of war.

The battalion advanced to LeFret and aided in its capture; an additional 1,600 Allied prisoners were set free. On September 19 they were relieved from duty at LeFret and assembled at Prat Meaur. Throughout the rest of September the battalion moved from town to town. To their disappointment, they did not make it to Paris.

Their most difficult and longest days actually occurred six months after D-Day from December 5-8, '44. They were ordered to Bergsten, Germany, to set up a defensive perimeter around the town. Near the village a hill rose about 400 feet. They called it "Hill 400." It was the most significant observation post for the Germans in the Roer Valley of the Hurtgen Forrest.

Companies D and F made a reconnaissance and assaulted "Hill 400." The two companies captured the hill, but the Germans laid down a heavy artillery and mortar barrage. D and F Companies dug in on the hill. The Rangers held back several intense counterattacks. In the town the other Ranger companies also repulsed German counterattacks, and by December 8, 3d Battalion, 13th Infantry Regiment, reached the area to relieve the sorely outnumbered 2d Rangers.[2] Rudder's men again paid a heavy price in casualties during the battle for "Hill 400."

Between D-Day and the end of the war, the 2d Rangers fought through five countries: France, Belgium, Germany, Czechoslovakia and Luxembourg.[3] They participated in seven invasions, 26 major battles, and 14 campaigns.[4] On May 11, 1945, the 2d Ranger Battalion was stationed in Czechoslovakia when they heard the news of the German surrender. The men assembled for the last time. They were happy to be going home, but they knew it was the end of their wartime brotherhood. They soon, however, learned that Ranger friendships last forever, even in peace time.

Herm Stein, F Company, recalled: "There were only two times that I wept in depression, once in a service to our fallen comrades — I went thinking of Jack Richards — and the other, when the outfit . . . was split up at Newport News, Virginia. I had to bid my final adieu to L-Rod; I was so thankful and glad to get home but part of me was . . ." devastated. Rudder's Rangers were no more.[5]

Notes to Chapter 19

[1] Haggerty, 246.
[2] For a complete history of HQ Company and the 2d Rangers after D-Day see Clark, *2nd Ranger Battalion: The Narrative History of Headquarters Company,* 64-100.
[3] Elder, 5.
[4] Leonard Lomell's speech, May 8, 1995, at Eisenhower Center, New Orleans, page 2.
[5] Herman Stein's account of the battle, transcript supplied by Herman Stein on June 17, 1999.

Appendix I

In 1945 the United States Government recognized the 2d Ranger Battalion for their bravery during June 6-8, 1944. The following is the citation given to the unit.

General Orders

No. 10

February 1945

War Department

Washington 25, D.C., 22

The 2d Ranger Infantry Battalion is cited for outstanding performance of duty in action. In the invasion of France the 2d Ranger Infantry Battalion was assigned the mission of securing two separate sectors of the beachhead. Three companies of the battalion landed on the beach at Pointe du Hoc, Normandy, France, at 0630, 6 June 1944, under concentrated rifle, machine-gun, artillery, and rocket fire of the enemy. The companies faced not only terrific enemy fire but also mines and hazardous underwater and beach obstacles. Despite numerous casualties suffered in the landing, these companies advanced and successfully assaulted cliffs 100 feet in height. By grim determination and extraordinary heroism, large enemy coastal guns which had been interdicting the beach with constant shell fire were reached and destroyed. At the same time, the remainder of the battalion landed on the beach at Vierville-sur-Mur at 0630, 6 June 1944, directly under withering enemy rifle, machine-gun, artillery, and rocket fire. These companies suffered heavy casualties. Yet such was their gallantry and heroism that they would not be stopped in their advance, and destroy a coastal battery of large enemy guns. This action secured the necessary beachhead for the forces that were to follow. The outstanding determination and esprit de corps of the 2d Rangers Infantry Battalion, in the face of tremendous odds, are in keeping with the highest traditions of the service.

By order of the Secretary of War:

G. C. Marshall
Chief of Staff

The Liberation of Pointe du Hoc

Appendix II

Roster of Cos. D, E, F, and HQ, 2d Ranger Battalion as of June 6, 1944, compiled from Roland Rowe's Coll., 2d Ranger Battalion Box, USAMHI Archives.

Key: KIA= Killed in Action
WIA=Wounded in Action
LWA=Lightly wounded in action
SWA=Severely wounded in action

Unit: Headquarters

	Boat Team	Status
Lt. Col. James Rudder	888	Wounded three times, Survived
Lt. Col. George S. Williams		Survived
Lt. Col. Travis Trevor,	722	British Commando, Wounded, survived
Maj. Edgar L. Arnold		Survived
Capt. Walter Block, battalion doctor		Killed, at a later time
Capt. Harvey J. Cook		Survived
Capt. James A. Malaney		Survived
Capt. Richard P. Merrill		Survived
Capt. Frederick G. Wilkin		SWA
Lt. Jame R. McCullers	DUKW	WIA, survived
Lt. William Heaney		Survived
Lt. Elmer Vermeer		Engineer, survived
Lt. G.K. Hodenfield	883	Stars and Stripes reporter, survived

Headquarters Company:

	Boat Team	Status
Lt. James "Ike" W. Eikner	888	Survived
1st Sgt. John Erderly		Survived
M/Sgt. Robert Lemin		Supply boat KIA
T/Sgt. Edward Gurney		Intelligence & Operation, Survived
T/Sgt. John V. Koepfer		Survived
T/Sgt. Francis J. Roach		Communications Survived

Headquarters Company Continued:

	Boat Team	Status
S/Sgt. Otto C. Bayer		Medic, survived
S/Sgt. Colin J. Lowe		Survived
S/Sgt. Donald F. Mentzer		Medic, survived
T/3 Randall R. Rinker		Survived
Sgt. William I. Mollohan, Jr.	Supply boat	KIA
T/4 Stephen Liscinsky	722	Radioman, survived
T/4 Charles S. Parker	722	Radioman, survived
T/4 Frank E. South		Medic, survived
Cpl. Lou Lisko	722	Radioman, survived
T/5 William C. Clark, Jr.		Survived
T/5 Gerald A. Eberle		I & O, survived
T/5 Louis Herman		Radioman, MIA at sea
T/5 Virgil A. Hillis		Survived
T/5 Edward A. Johnson		Comm, survived
T/5 Francis Kolodziejczak		
T/5 Robert C. Lambert		Medic
T/5 Steve N. Mead		Transport, MIA
T/5 Marcel Miller		Radioman, survived
Pfc. John R. Ahart	DUKW	MIA, survived
Pfc. Thomas J. Armbruster	DUKW	Survived
Pfc. Eugene C. Doughty	DUKW	Survived
Pfc. George A. Hall	DUKW	Survived
Pfc. James A. Machan		Radioman, KIA
Pfc. Theodore A. Malburg, Jr.		MIA, survived
Pfc. Robert F. Shirey		Communications, survived
Pfc. Guy C. Shoaf		Survived
Pfc. Billy Tibbets	DUKW	Survived
Pfc. John W. Tindell	DUKW	MIA, survived
Pfc. Kenneth L. Wharff	I & O,	MIA, survived
Pvt. Rolland Revels	DUKW	KIA
Pvt. Robert K. Roe		Communications, survived
Pvt. William F. Sluss	DUKW	KIA

293rd Joint Assault Signal Company

	Boat Team	Status
Capt. Jonathan H. Harwood		KIA
Lt. Bennie Berger (USN)		Survived
Lt. Kenneth S. Norton (USN)		KIA
Lt. Sylvester J. Varuska		Survived
Sgt. Joseph J. Groth		Survived
T/5 Herman W. Calmes		Survived
T/5 Edward G. Heineck		Survived
Pfc. Jerome O. Abare		Survived
Pfc. Alvert Kamente		Survived
Pfc. William J. Skelly		Survived
Pvt. Charles C. Arvizu		Survived
Pvt. Wallace M. Crank		Survived
Pvt. Howard J. Ericson		Survived
Pvt. Irvin H. Ferriera		Survived
Pvt. Arthur E. Gamble		Survived
Pvt. John Gallagher		Survived
Pvt. Henry W. Genther		KIA
Pvt. Mitchell H. Goldenstein		Survived
Pvt. Francis Jakowski		Survived
Pvt. Paul E. Kimbrough		Survived

165th Signal Photo Co:

		Status
Lt. Amos P. Potts		Survived
Sgt. Warden F. Lovell		Survived
T/4 Irving Lomasky		KIA
Pfc. Kegham Nigohosian		KIA

Company D: LCA 860, LCA 668, LCA 858

	Boat Team	Status
Capt. Harold Slater	860	Officially transferred to HQ Co. just prior to D-Day. His boat sunk off shore, rescued
Lt. Morten McBride	860	Listed MIA, later accounted for
Lt. George Kerchner	858	Survived
1st Sgt. Leonard Lomell	668	WIA, survived
T/Sgt. Richard Spleen		Captured, survived
T/Sgt. Harvey Koenig	668	SWA, survived

T/Sgt. John Corona	860	MIA, survived
S/Sgt. Jack Kuhn	668	Survived
S/Sgt. Patrick McCrone	668	KIA-6-6-44
S/Sgt. Francis Pacyga	668	SWA, survived
S/Sgt. Charles Kettering	668	KIA
S/Sgt. Sigurd Sunby	668	Survived
S/Sgt. Norman Miller	860	KIA
S/Sgt. Joseph Stevens	860	MIA, survived
S/Sgt. Melvin Sweany		Survived
S/Sgt. Joseph Flanagan		KIA, at a later date
S/Sgt. Lawrence Johnson		KIA, 6-7-44
S/Sgt. Benjamin Wirtz		KIA, at a later date
S/Sgt. Lester Arthur		Died in hospital, 6-14-44
Sgt. Micheal Branley		WIA, survived but killed at a later date
Sgt. Robert Austin		KIA at a later date
Sgt. Lester Harris	668	Suvived
Sgt. Kelly Szowesuk		KIA
Sgt. Richard McLaughlin		MIA, 6-7-44, survived
Sgt. Harry Fate		Survived
Sgt. Emory Jones		MIA, 6-7-44, killed at a later date
Sgt. Joseph Devoli	860	MIA, 6-6-44, survived
Sgt. Morris Webb		SWA, survived
Cpl. Maurice R. Browning		KIA
T/5 Robert Wells		MIA, survived
T/5 William H. Graham		KIA
T/5 Raymond Riendeau	860	KIA, drowned
T/5 Clarence J. Long		KIA
T/5 Clinton Hensley		MIA,6-6-44, survived
T/5 William Vaughan	668	KIA
T/5 John Clifton		KIA
T/5 Harvey R. Huff		Survived
T/5 Louis J. Bisek		MIA, 6-6-44, survived
T/5 Ed Secor		MIA, 6-6-44, survived
T/5 Henry Stecki		MIA, 6-7-44, survived

Company D, continued	Boat Team	Status
T/5 William A. Walker		MIA, 6-6-44, survived
T/5 Gordon Luning		Survived
T/5 Thomas Mendenhall	860	KIA
T/5 George Schnelle		SWA, survived
Pfc. James Blum		MIA, 6-7-44, KIA undetermined
Pfc. John J. Riley	914 (supply boat)	MIA, survived
Pfc. Steve Sezephanski		SWA
Pfc. Robert Fruhling	860	WIA, survived
Pfc. Miljavac		KIA
Pfc. William Cruz	858	LWA, survived
Pfc. Sheldon Bare		WIA, survived
Pfc. James Hudnell		MIA, 6-6-44, survived
Pfc. Williams		MIA, 6-6-44, survived
Pfc. Harold E. Lester	860	KIA
Pfc. Peter Korpalo		MIA, 6-6-44, survived
Pfc. William K. Hoffman		Survived
Pfc. Domonic Sparaco	860	MIA, 6-6-44, survived
Pfc. Leonard Rubin	668	MIA, 6-7-44, survived
Pfc. John D. Oehlberg	914 (supply boat)	KIA
Pfc. Alvin H. Nance	668	MIA, survived
Pfc. Anthony J. Ruggiero	860	MIA, 6-6-44, survived
Pfc. Melvin C. Hoffelbower, Jr.		KIA
Pfc. McCorkle		KIA, 6-8-44
Pfc. Lester Harris		SWA, survived
Pfc. Jack Conaboy		SWA, survived
Pfc. Leroy G. Adams		KIA, at a later time
Pfc. Robert C. Carty		KIA, 6-7-44
Pfc. Iriving Hoover	860	Survived
Pvt. Henry Sobal		Survived
T/5 William A. Geitz (HQ Co.)	668	Attachedto company as medic, detached 6-21-44, survived

Company E: LCA 861, LCA 862, LCA 888 (including HQ personnel), LCA 722 (including HQ personnel)

	Boat Team	Status
1st Lt. Theodore E. Lapres	861	Survived
Lt. Joseph E. Leagans	862	KIA, 6-7-44
Lt. Gilbert C. Baugh		LWA
Lt. Frank L. Kennard		Survived
1st Sgt. Robert W. Lang	888	Survived
T/Sgt. Clifford E. Mains		Captured, survived
T/Sgt. Harold W. Gunthur	861	Survived
T/Sgt. Lawrence Lare		Survived
T/Sgt. Millard W. Hayden		KIA
T/Sgt. Hayward Robey	722	Survived
S/Sgt. Christopher M. Anderson		SWA
S/Sgt. Robert S. Pyles		SWA
S/Sgt. Robert A. Honhart		Survived
S/Sgt. Joseph J. Cleaves	862	SWA
S/Sgt. Charles H. Denbo	861	SWA
S/Sgt. Glen L. Webster		Survived
S/Sgt. Curtis A. Simmons	861	KIA
S/Sgt. Frank A. Rupinski		MIA, 6-9-44, survived
S/Sgt. Rex D. Clark		Survived
S/Sgt. Earl A. Theobald		Survived
Sgt. Andrew T. Yardley	861	Survived
Sgt. Anthony P. Catelani		MIA, 6-9-44, survived
Sgt. Domenick B. Boggetto	888	MIA, 6-9-44, survived
Sgt. Aloysius S. Nosal		MIA, 6-9-44, survived
Sgt. Harry G. Fritchman, Jr.		MIA, 6-9-44, survived
Sgt. Theodore M. Pilalas	DUK	MIA, 6-8-44, survived
T/5 Edward P. Smith	722	Survived
T/5 Leroy J. Thompson	862	SWA, 6-7-44, survived
T/5 Mike Milkovich, Jr.		Survived
T/5 George J. Putzek		SWA, survived
T/5 Albert J. Uronis		
T/5 Frank J. La Brandt		MIA, 6-9-44
T/5 Kenneth H. Bargmann		MIA, 6-9-44, survived

T/5 E.G. Colvard	861	SWA
T/5 Charles G. McCalvin		KIA
T/5 Paul P. Knor	DUKW	MIA
Pfc. John S. Burnett		MIA, 6-8-44, survived
Pfc. Paul L. Medeiros	861	SWA, survived
Pfc. Howard Bowens		KIA
Pfc. George W. Mackey	861	KIA
Pfc. Salva P. Maimone		MIA, 6-9-44, survived
Pfc. Roy L. Palmer		MIA, 6-9-44
Pfc. Charles H. Bellows, Jr.	862	KIA
Pfc. Anton Bachleda		SWA
Pfc. Shalaim		
Pfc. Clarence E. Bachman, Jr.		Survived
Pfc. Frank H. Peterson	722	SWA, survived
Pfc. Nathan C. Reed		SWA, survived
Pfc. John C. Sillmon		SWA, survived
Pfc. Harry W. Roberts	861	LWA/SWA, 6-8-44, survived
Pfc. Henry A. Wood		LWA/MIA, 6-9-44, killed
Pfc. Victor J. Aguzzi	862	Survived
Pfc. George H. Crook		MIA, 6-9-44, survived
Pfc. Joseph J. Lock		MIA, 6-9-44, survived
Pfc. Harold D. Main		SWA,6-7-44, survived
Pfc. Woodrow Talkington		SWA, 6-7-44, survived
Pfc. Wadsworth		WIA/SWA, 6-9-44
Pfc. Jack Lawson, Jr.		
Pfc. Edison W. Crull		KIA, at a later time
Pfc. Roe		Detached
Pfc. Francis J. Connolly	914 (supply boat)	KIA, 6-8-44
Pfc. Duncan N. Daugherty	DUKW	SWA, survived
Pfc. Richard Hubbard	DUKW	MIA, 6-8-44
Pfc. Ralph E. Davis	888	
Pfc. William D. Bell	861	Survived
Pfc. Charles M. Dunlap		Survived
Pfc. Mark A. Keefer, Jr.		
Pvt. Frank B. Robinson		MIA, 6-9-44
Pvt. Harold W. Sehorn		MIA, 6-9-44
Pfc. Michael J. McDonough (HQ Company)		Attached to company as medic/detached 6-21-44, survived

Company F: LCA 883, LCA 884, LCA 887

	Boat Team	Status
Capt. Otto Masny	883	LWA, survived
Lt. Jacob J. Hill	884	KIA
Lt. Robert C. Arman	887	Survived
Lt. Richard A. Wintz	883	Survived
Lt. John W. White		Survived
1st Sgt. Charles E. Frederick		Survived
T/Sgt. John W. Franklin		Survived
T/Sgt. Bonnie M. Taylor		Survived
T/Sgt. Eugene E. Elder		Survived
T/Sgt. William "L-Rod" Petty	887	WIA, survived
T/Sgt. John I. Cripps	887	Survived
S/Sgt. Robert G. Youso	883	WIA, survived
S/Sgt. William Stivison	DUKW	Survived
S/Sgt. Carl Bombardier	884	Survived
S/Sgt. Thomas F. Ryan		Survived
S/Sgt. Carl Weilage		urvived
S/Sgt. James E. Fulton	884	WIA, 6-8-44, survived
S/Sgt. Paul P. Welsch		Survived
S/Sgt. Bill L. Thompson		Survived
S/Sgt. Leon Otto	884	Mortally wounded
S/Sgt. Harry J. Ferry		Wounded, survived
S/Sgt. Vergil L. Longest		Survived
S/Sgt. William H. Simons		WIA, survived
S/Sgt. William J. Uhorczuk		Survived
Sgt. Regis McCloskey	Supply boat	WIA, survived
Sgt. James R. Alexander	887	MIA, 6-7-44, survived
Sgt. Murrell F. Stinnette		KIA later
Sgt. Robert G. Roosa		Survived
Sgt. Jack H. Richards	883	KIA
Sgt. Leonard F. Zajas		Survived
Sgt. William M. McHugh	887	Survived
T/5 Glen J. Swafford		Survived
T/5 Floyd H. Simkins		MIA, 6-7-44, survived
T/5 Orley R. Jackson		Survived
T/5 Herman Stein	883	Survived
T/5 Charles J. Vella		KIA later
Pfc. William F. O'Keefe		Survived
Pfc. Dennis F. Kimble		KIA
Pfc. Garness L. Colden	887	KIA later

Pfc. John Bacho	884	WIA, survived
Pfc. Raymond A. Cole	883	KIA
Pfc. William D. Walsh		WIA, survived
Pfc. George A. Wieburg		KIA
Pfc. Gerald A. Bouchard		WIA, survived
Pfc. Frederick A. Dix	887	WIA, survived
Pfc. Alvin E. White	883	WIA, survived
Pfc. Jack W. Lamero		KIA, at a later time
Pfc. Madison B. Cobb		WIA, survived
Pfc. Oscar E. Behrent		Survived
Pfc. Walter T. Bialkowski		Survived
Pfc. Walter J. Borowski		Survived
Pfc. William H. Coldsmith	887	Survived
Pfc. William A. Gervais		Survived
Pfc. John J. Gilhooly	DUKW	Survived
Pfc. Herman W. Kiihnl		Survived
Pfc. Robert G. Landin	887	Survived
Pfc. Robert E. McKittrick		Survived
Pfc. Cloise A. Manning		Survived
Pfc. Edward J. Trombowicz		Survived
Pfc. Frank J. Oropello		Survived
Pfc. Donald C. Pechacek		Survived
Pfc. Rudolph Stefik		Survived
Pfc. Jean N. Ver Schave		Survived
Pfc. Carl Winsch	887	Survived
Pvt. William F. Anderson	884	Killed at a later time
Pvt. James E. Kohl		Survived
T/5 Robert E. Gillespie (HQ Company)		Attached, survived
T/5 Ralph E. Davis (HQ Company)		Attached as medic, survived
T/5 Charles W. Korb (HQ Company)		Supply boat, Attached, as medic/WIA, survived

Appendix III

Killed In Action
June 6-8, 1944

Headquarters Company:

M/Sgt. Robert Lemin
Sgt. William L. Mollohan, Jr.
Pfc. James A. Machan
Pvt. Rolland Revels
Pvt. William F. Sluss

293rd Jnt. Assault Sig. Co:
Capt. Jonathan H. Harwood
Lt. Kenneth S. Norton, (USN)
Pvt. Henry W. Genther

165th Sig. Photo Co:
T/4 Irving Lomasky
Pfc. Kegham Nigohosian

E Company:
Lt. Joseph E. Leagans
T/Sgt. Millard W. Hayden
S/Sgt. Curtis A. Simmons
T/5 Charles G. McCalvin
Pfc. Howard Bowens
Pfc. George W. Mackey
Pfc. Charles H. Bellows, Jr.
Pfc. Henry A. Wood
Pfc. Francis J. Connolly

D Company:

S/Sgt. Patrick McCrone
S/Sgt. Charles Kettering
S/Sgt. Norman Miller
S/Sgt. Lawrence Johnson
S/Sgt. Lester Arthur,
  mortally wounded died June 14.
Sgt. Kelly Szowesuk
T/5 Raymond Riendeau
T/5 Clarence J. Long
T/5 John Clifton
T/5 Thomas Mendenhall
Pfc. Miljavac
Pfc. Harold E. Lester
Pfc. John D. Oehlberg
Pfc. Melvin C. Hoffelbower, Jr.
Pfc. McCorkle
Pfc. Robert C. Carty
Pfc. James Blum

F Company:
Lt. Jacob Hill
S/Sgt. Leon Otto
Sgt. Jack Richards
Pfc. Dennis Kimble
Pfc. Raymond A. Cole
Pfc. George A. Wieburg

Appendix IV

Recipients of the Distinguished Service Cross

The following men who fought on the Pointe and received the second highest award the military bestows, the Distinguished Service Cross. Surprisingly, the U.S. Military never awarded any World War II Ranger the Medal of Honor, their reason being there were not enough witnesses. The Army did, however, award all the members of the 2d Ranger Battalion — the killed and the survivors — the Bronze Service Arrowhead for participation in the Normandy Invasion of D-Day, June 6, 1944.

Lt. Col. James E. Rudder, CO
Lt. George Kerchner, D Company
Sgt. Leonard Lomell, D Company
Sgt. Warden F. Lovell, 165th Sig. Photo Co.
Capt. Otto Masny, F Company
T/Sgt. John W. White, F Company

JoAnna McDonald

Bibliography

Unpublished Primary Accounts:

Telephone Interviews:

James W. Eikner, July 25, 1999
Gene Elder, June 1999
George Kerchner, August 15 & August 17, 1999
Jack Kuhn, July 1999
Leonard Lomell, July 1999, August 13 & August 15, 1999
Herman Stein, June and July 1999

Personal Papers and Manuscripts:

Black, Robert. Ranger Battalion Box, 2d Ranger folder. United States Army Military History Institute, Carlisle, Pennsylvania.

Brown, Owen L. Oral History Transcript, supplied by the Eisenhower Center, New Orleans, Louisiana.

Chapelie, Sylvie. *The American Example Overlord.* Testimony and Interviews of Lt. G. K. Hodenfield and Cpl. Lou Lisko.

Eikner, James W. Oral History Transcript, supplied by the Eisenhower Center, New Orleans, Louisiana.

____. Letter detailing his life sent to the author June 30, 1999.

____. Packet including maps, his slide show presentation which he gives to school children and veteran organizations. Sent to author on July 12, 1999.

Elder, Gene. Oral History Transcript, Eisenhower Center, New Orleans, Louisiana.

Kerchner, George. Oral History Transcript, Eisenhower Center, New Orleans, Louisiana.

____. Personal diary kept from June 6-14, 1944. Copy supplied by George Kerchner.

Lisko, Ruth. Letter to the author written by Ruth, wife of Lou Lisko, September 1998.

Lisko, Louis F. Papers at the United States Army Military History Institute, Archives Section

Lomell, Leonard. Personal interview with Len Lomell, August 22, 1999.

____ Oral History Transcript, Eisenhower Center, New Orleans, Louisiana.

____. Packet sent by Lomell to author July 1999. Includes maps, photos and articles about 2d Ranger Battalion.

____. Transcript of speech given May 17, 1999, *Recollections of WWII: D-Day and the Rangers of Normandy, France.*

Raaen, John J., Jr. Oral History Transcript, Eisenhower Center, New Orleans, Louisiana.

South, Frank. Oral History Transcript, Eisenhower Center, New Orleans, Louisiana.

____. World War II survey. Ranger Box, USAMHI Archives.

The Liberation of Pointe du Hoc

Stein, Herman. Account of battle sent to the author June 1999.
Vermeer, Elmer. Description and account of the battle. Roland Rowe Collection, USAMHI Archives.
Walsh, Bill, Jr. Letter to the author dated January 13, 1999.

Published Primary Sources:

Baer, Alfred E., Jr. *D for Dog: The Story of a Ranger Company.* Memphis, Tennessee, 1946.
Churchill, Winston. *Their Finest Hour.* Boston, Massachusetts: Houghton Mifflin Company, 1949.
Combined Operations Pamphlets. September 1942.
Darby, William O. and William H. Baumer. *Darby's Rangers: We Led the Way.* San Rafael, California: Presidio Press, 1980.
_____. "U.S. Rangers." n.p., 1944. Lecture Army and Navy College, Washington, D.C., October 27, 1944.
Eikner, James W. "Rangers can do the job." *The Houston Post.* Tuesday, June 5, 1984, 3B.
_____. Project compiled by Clark, George M., William Weber and Ronald Paradis. *2nd Ranger Bn: The Narrative History of Headquarters Company April 1943-May 1945.* n.d.
Ewing, Joseph H. *29 Let's Go! A History of the 29th Infantry Division in World War II.* Washington, D.C.: Infantry Journal Press, 1948.
Heinz, W. C. "I took My Son to Omaha Beach." *Colliers.* June 11, 1954, 21-28.
Salmon, Sidney. *2nd U.S. Rangers Infantry Battalion.* Doylestown, Pennsylvania: Birchwood Books, 1991.
Sovisto, Edwin M. *2nd Ranger Battalion: Roughing It with Charlie.* Williamstown, New Jersey: Antietam National Museum. n.d.
Truscott, Lt. Gen. Lucian K., Jr. *Command Missions: A Personal Story.* New York, New York: P. Dutton and Co., 1954.
U.S. Army Historical Section Staff, Historical Division. *Omaha Beachhead: June 6-13, 1944.* Nashville, Tennessee: Battery Press, 1984.
U.S. Army Historical Section Staff, Historical Division. *Small Unit Actions: France: 2d Ranger Battalion at Pointe du Hoc; Saipan: 27th Division on Tanapag Plain; Italy: 351st Infantry at Santa Maria Infante; France: 4th Armored Division at Singling.* Washington, D. C.: War Department Historical Division, 1946.
U.S. Army Historical Section Staff, Historical Division. *The War In Western Europe.* Part I (June to December, 1944.) Department of Military Art and Engineering: United States Military Academy, West Point, New York, 1952.

Published Secondary Sources:
Articles:

"American Rangers from the Colonial Era to the Present," *Rangers.* October 1, 1984.
Barnicle, Mike. D-Day: The Heroes Remembered/The Countryside;

Commentary." *The Boston Globe.* June 7, 1994.

Blair, Sam. "Rudder's Rangers: Texan's Leadership Shone in Daring D-Day Assault; Charge Silenced Guns to Assist Allies' Victory." *The Dallas Morning News,* June 5, 1994.

Burney, Joan. "50 Years Later, Family sees Cliffs D-Day Survivor Once Scaled." *Omaha World Herald.* September 6, 1994.

Dobbs, Michael. Reagan to Visit Site of Ranger Assault; aged veteran climbs cliff to relive D-Day drama." *The Washington Post.* June 6, 1984.

Drell, Adrienne. Rangers' Second Landing a Real Fete." *Chicago Sun-Times.* June 5, 1994.

Hunter, Stephen. War Movie Still Falls Short, but Hollywood brings it back for a victorious stand on video." *The Baltimore Sun.* June 6, 1994.

Johnson, Thomas M. "The Army's Fightingest Outfit Comes Home." *Reader's Digest.* December 1944, 51-54.

Lehman, Milton. The Rangers Fought Ahead of Everybody." *The Saturday Evening Post.* June 15, 1946.

Locke, Peter. Hard-Hitting Commandos." *New York Times Magazine.* April 5, 1942, 6-7, 33.

MacDonald, Charles B. World War II: The War Against Germany and Italy." *American Military History.* Washington, D.C.: U.S. Army, 1989.

Marshall, S.L.A. "First Wave at Omaha Beach." *Atlantic Monthly.* Vol. 206, #5. November 1960, 67-72.

Mahon, John K. "Anglo-American Methods of Indian Warfare." *Mississippi Valley Historical Review*, 1958.

Morris, Sgt. Mack. "Rangers Come Home and Bring Stories of Their Tough Campaigns in Africa and Europe." *Yank: The Army Weekly.* August 4, 1944, 3-5.

Templeton, "A Reluctant Hero." *Pittsburgh Post-Gazette.* June 5, 1994.

"The Rangers: Survivors of toughest, most bitterly lacerated U.S. infantry force are home for well-earned rest," *Life.* August 31, 1944, 59-63.

Thomas, Bruce. "The Commando." *Harper's Magazine.* March 1942, 438-440.

Books:

Altieri, James. *The Spearheaders.* New York, NY: The Bobb's-Merrill Co., Inc., 1960.

Ambrose, Stephen E. *D-Day, June 6, 1944: The Climactic Battle of World War II.* New York: Simon and Schuster, 1994.

Astor, Gerald. *June 6, 1944: The Voices of D-Day.* New York, New York: St. Martin's Press, 1994.

Balkoski, Joseph. *Beyond the Beachhead: The 29th Infantry Division in Normandy.* Mechanicsburg, Pennsylvania: Stackpole Publications, 1989, 1999.

Chandler, David G. and James Lawton Collins, Jr. *The D-Day Encylcopedia.* New York, New York: Simon and Schuster, 1994.

Cuneo, John R. *Robert Rogers of the Rangers.* New York, New York: Oxford University Press, 1959.

D'Este, Carlo. *Decision in Normandy: The Unwritten Story of Montgomery and the Allied Campaign.* London: Collins, 1983.

Drez, Ronald. *Voices of D-Day.* Baton Rouge, Louisiana: Louisiana State University Press, 1994.

Edell, Ed. *A Special Breed of Man.* Guilderland, New York: Ranger Associates, Inc., 1984.

Farrow, Edward S. *A Dictionary of Military Terms.* New York, New York: Crowell Publishers, 1918.

Glassman, Henry. *"Lead the Way, Rangers:" A History of the Fifth Ranger Battalion.* Germany, 1945.

Harrison, Gordon A. *United States Army In World War II: The European Theater of Operations Cross-Channel Attack.* Washington, D.C.: U.S. Department of the Army, 1951.

Historical Sub-Section, Supreme Headquarters, Allied Expeditionary Force, *History of COSSAC, 1943-1944.*

Hogan, David W. *Raiders or Elite Infantry?: The Changing Role of the U.S. Army Rangers from Dieppe to Grenada.* Westport, Connecticut: Greenwood Press, 1992

_____. *U.S. Army Special Operations in World War II.* Washington, D.C.: Department of the Army, 1992.

Keegan, John. *Six Armies in Normandy: From D-Day to the Liberation of Paris, June 6th, 1944-August 25th, 1944.* London: Jonathan Cape, 1982.

King, Michael J. *William Orlando Darby: A Military Biography.* Hamden, Connecticut, Archon Books, 1981.

_____. *Rangers: Selected Combat Operations in World War II.* Leavenworth Papers no. 11. Fort Leavenworth, Kansas: Command and General Staff College, 1985.

Ladd, James. *Commandos and Rangers of World War II.* London: MacDonald and Jane's, 1978.

Lane, Ronald L. *Rudder's Rangers.* Manassas, Virginia: Ranger Associates, 1979.

MacDonald, Charles B. *The Mighty Endeavor: The American War In Europe.* New York, New York: Morrow, 1969.

Mosby, John S. *Mosby's War Reminiscence.* New York, New York: Pageant Book Co., 1958.

Partridge, Eric. *Origins: A Short Etymological Dictionary of Modern English.* New York, New York: MacMillan, 1963.

Pogue, Forrest C. *The Supreme Command.* Washington, D.C.: U.S. Army, 1954.

Rosignoli, Guido. *Army Basges and Insignia of World War II.* New York, MacMillan, 1972.

Ryan, Cornelius. *The Longest Day: The Classic Epic of D-Day June 6, 1944.* New York, New York: Touchstone, 1959.

U.S. War Department. *Handbook on German Military Forces.* Baton Rouge: Louisiana State University Press, 1990.

Webb, Walter. *The Texas Rangers.* 2d ed. Boston, Massachusetts: Houghton Mifflin Company, 1965.

Dissertations:

Haggerty, Jerome J. "A History of the Ranger Battalions In World War II." Fordham University, New York, 1982.

Hogan, David W. "The Evolution of the Concept of the U.S. Army's Rangers." Duke University, North Carolina, 1986.

Index

Weber, T/4 William, 22, 57
Weymouth, England, 57
White, Pvt. Alvin, 87
Williams, Capt. George S., 27
Winsch, T/5 Carl, 84, 94, 148
Wintz, Lt. Richard A., 85, 87, 98, 121-122, 124, 158
Yardley, Sgt. Andrew J., 104-106
Youso, Sgt. Robert, 87
Zages, Pvt. Lester, 151